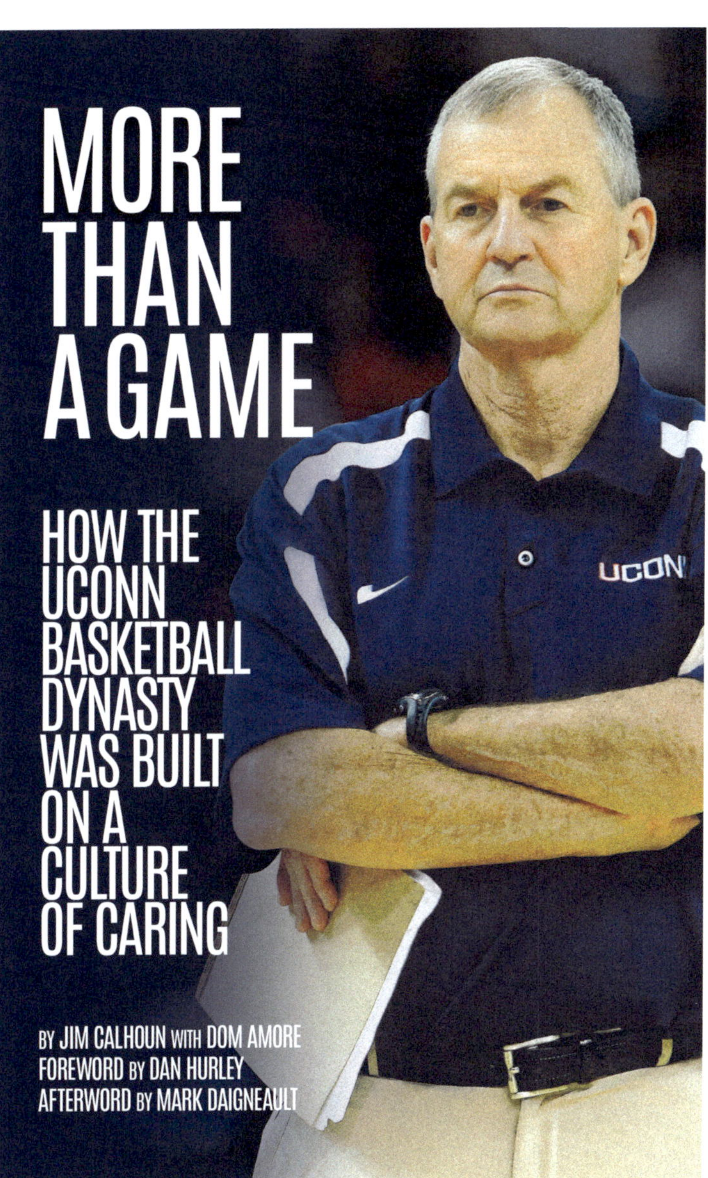
MORE THAN A GAME
HOW THE UCONN BASKETBALL DYNASTY WAS BUILT ON A CULTURE OF CARING
UCONN
BY JIM CALHOUN WITH DOM AMORE
FOREWORD BY DAN HURLEY
AFTERWORD BY MARK DAIGNEAULT

MORE THAN A GAME

HOW THE UCONN BASKETBALL DYNASTY WAS BUILT UPON A CULTURE OF CARING

JIM CALHOUN WITH DOM AMORE

Woodhall Press | Norwalk, CT

Woodhall Press, Norwalk, CT 06855
WoodhallPress.com

Cover design: LJ Mucci
Layout artist: LJ Mucci

Library of Congress Cataloging-in-Publication Data available

ISBN 978-1-960456-45-8 (paper: alk paper)
ISBN 978-1-960456-46-5 (electronic)

First Edition
Distributed by Independent Publishers Group
(800) 888-4741

Printed in the United States of America

CONTENTS

Jim Calhoun and Dan Hurley celebrate UConn's sixth national championship.

Credit: UConn Athletics

FOREWORD

"When Coach Calhoun Loves, He Loves Hard"

By Dan Hurley

The excitement from my introductory press conference at UConn had died down, and it was time to get down to work. I compare repairing a basketball program to fixing an automobile. You don't really know how much fixing it needs until you open the hood.

The first few days, first few practices, were a disaster. You could say I was having buyer's remorse about leaving Rhode Island.

I knew Coach Calhoun, who was still contributing at the university, was in his office down the hall from mine, and I walked down there looking for somewhere to vent, to commiserate, coach-to-coach.

You lift up the hood and you've got all these issues, I started to tell him. You've got talent issues, you've got behavioral issues, you've got issues academically, just a culture that eroded from what the program once was in a very significant way. I was down. I was tired from the season, I was tired from rebuilding Rhode Island. And now you go on this whirlwind to a new job and you realize the amount of work you have in front of you. This was before NIL, before the transfer portal, so you knew it was going to be a heck of a battle.

I actually went in there thinking coach would be in agreement with me, empathize and make me feel better, say, "Hey, I know, right, yeah. This thing is really in bad shape, Dan, you've got it so tough..." But as I vented, I could see his face changing. The expression went from listening to what I had to say to disdain...then a little bit of disgust...then a little bit of, "are you serious?" You're not who I thought you were. Are you kidding? What did we hire you to do here?'

Coach was seventy-six, had retired as coach six years earlier, but he loved UConn, was proud of the championship culture he had built from nothing, and I was to learn, as so many of his players had: When Coach Calhoun loves, he loves hard.

I mean, he really ripped me.

"You hired your staff, right, Coach?" he barked. "You hired your staff, right?" (With maybe some expletives in there.) "Well, go and tell you freaking Athletic Director and tell him what you need to get this thing fixed and get us back where we belong. Don't feel sorry for yourself. What did we get here?" When I mentioned that the weights in our weight room were a few years old, he said, dripping sarcasm, "Oh? I didn't know weights wore out." He told me to stop being a baby.

I kind of rolled out of his office, a little shell-shocked. I walked back down the hallway, got the staff together, called my agent, called our Athletic Director, David Benedict, and got my act together. "Hey, Dave, we need this, this, this and this." To my assistants: "Guys, wake up. We need to get better players in here. Who's the first commit we're going to get?"

It was a jump start. I was like a car, I needed cables. Coach Calhoun was the man to get under my hood and provide the jolt I needed.

The first time I remember seeing Coach was at ABCD camp back, about 30 years earlier, when it was held at Princeton. I was just a high school player; you'd be playing in the All-America camp, and all these coaches, Bobby Knight and Coach K and P. J. Carlesimo and Jim Calhoun were leaning over the railing watching Court 3, larger than life.

Then Tate George announced he was going to UConn. He was a big New Jersey player when he committed. There were not a lot of big-time players going to Connecticut from the New York–New Jersey area at that time. It was like, wow, the best player in New Jersey just went to Connecticut. What is that?

A few years later, I was a freshman at Seton Hall, and I shared the court with Coach Calhoun as a player. I just remember this intense, kind of force-of-nature on the sideline who showed up with his Huskies, with the busses of fans, and he slapped the 2-2-1 press with 6-foot-7 Scott Burrell, future NBA champ, at the front of it. That was my introduction to Coach. He did not mingle or glad-hand opposing players.

We won that game, but I didn't get a shot off. UConn was on the way up, they were the upstart and you could feel it.

Once I got into coaching, I got every championship coaching video, went to any clinic within a reasonable area where I could see Coach. I tried to get there and learn as much as I could. I studied and tried to implement a lot of things.

When I was at Rhode Island, I hired Tom Moore, who had been assistant for two championships at UConn, and Tom invited Coach Calhoun come to a practice during my last season there.

When that practice was over, I got the chance to kind of pick his brain about my team and the things he liked, the things he didn't like, and he laid those things out in a real honest way. "Hey, your ball pressure sucks... You don't run the lanes the right way in transition." So I had that introduction with Coach and I got his phone number.

He had seen enough that he liked, I guess. He reached out to me when I was contemplating the move to UConn and offered his support that way, and through Tom Moore. "Take it, will you?" There might have been an expletive in here, too.

So following in Coach's footsteps at UConn means something to me. He had always been, along with my father, also a Hall-of-Famer, one of my coaching idols. How I approach things, how hard my teams play, my persona on the sidelines, how hard I coach my team, how hard we practice, I try to emulate a lot of what he did. And as time has gone on at UConn, and we succeeded in restoring the program to what it was during his time, national champions, he has stayed close to the program.

He watches every game, in person or on TV, and he frequently comes to practice for what I call "GOAT" talks, before a big game, before each stage of the NCAA Tournament. I have my superstitions, but his GOAT talks are not good luck charms.

The players see the bronze bust of him when they walk through the lobby of our practice facility, and they see the banners and we reference it all the time. And because he's close to us and we talk about our history so much, they have a better understanding than a lot of other kids their age. Their uncles, their dads, their high school coaches, AAU coaches, recognize him as one of the greatest ever to do it, Mount Rushmore, one of the greatest coaches ever, and that gets filtered to the players. They're a little bit in awe of him when he talks.

Now, in his eighties, when Coach comes in and addresses the team, he's still throwing heat, he's throwing 95 MPH. For seven years he has been mentoring me, taking the time to help me become a better coach and inspire me or give me great advice.

Or he'll tell me to get my head out of my backside. I've gotten tactical advice from him, I've gotten leadership and motivational advice from him, relative to team. I've gotten motivational, coach-to-coach advice from him, talent evaluation, with staff and players.

I grab a pen, one of these cards, and take notes. I'll ask him something. How did you motivate your staff? How did you stay on top of your staff so that they don't hate you but you keep them a little bit uncomfortable and you keep them on edge?

How did you teach this transition offense? No one got out on the break like his UConn teams. As player, as a fan, or at Wagner as a coach, I knew that team was on top of you. And he'll be, like, "we did this, here are the drills." And he's up on the whiteboard drawing it up.

He watches every game and he knows the team so well. He knows the personnel, he knows how we play because he comes to practice and he watches. I'll ask him, "Can you talk about these two or three things? Or address this one player?"

Going into the Final Four in 2023, Coach understood how important point guard play was going to be with Tristen Newton as we went for that first championship in Houston, with Miami and San Diego State our opponents. He addressed Tristen in the circle after practice. "Hey, man, you've got to play. This team, 2 through 5 are ready to win the national championship. You've gotta show up!" He brought up Kemba Walker's name and all the great point guards who have played at UConn, and T New went out and did it. Twice. He was the most outstanding player of our second championship, and is now with all those guards in the Huskies of Honor.

Coach has given me, passed on to me a belief in UConn, in who we are here and what we do, what we do in March, what we do in April, how we take the court, how we get after people, the way that we attack. I try to model all of that.

When Coach first came to UConn, they practiced in an old, dusty field house. But places don't win things. People do, men like him, men that are as relentless as he is, have obviously an incredible eye for talent, an eye for talent and team building, and build a team with incredible toughness and confidence and swagger. Intimidating defense. Intimidating in your face defensively and an attacking offense. Demand. A competitive rage, a relentlessness that ran through his teams and gave them this incredible armor of confidence when they got to Final Fours and national championship games.

Other teams felt the moment and got small in the moment, but his teams always played their best in championship moments because of how he toughened them up and put them in a position to play great and execute. How they attacked you. How relentless, ruthless they were.

He was the same way every single day, unrelenting in his standards and what he was going to hold his players to, his team to, a championship standard, an NBA standard. As a player, the level you had to perform for him on a daily basis, as a team, how you had to perform on a daily basis, or else he ripped you. Or just wouldn't allow it. He just wouldn't allow anyone to show up at less than their best on a daily basis, and that becomes your team.

And his players loved it from him. Great players want someone who is going to push them every day. Truly great players who can win big things for you and achieve great things in their career, they want a coach and a man like Coach Calhoun.

In this book, you will see how the UConn culture was built, that Coach loved hard. He loved his guys hard. He loved his players the way fathers loved their sons when he grew up. He held them accountable. He invested all of his time in them. He was the ultimate truth-teller. He pushed people beyond their level of comfort to be their best.

That is true love from a coach.

And on the flip side, if somebody gives you all of that, but sometimes maybe they lose their temper a little bit with you, maybe they're a little bit tougher on you, the benefits far outweigh it.

Is it uncomfortable at times? Absolutely. Are there days when they probably left the building in disgust with him? Couldn't stand him? Sure. But what he was doing for them was changing their lives.

Dan Hurley, fifty-two, has been UConn men's basketball head coach since 2018. He played for his father, Bob Hurley Sr., at famed St. Anthony's High in Jersey City, then at Seton Hall. He coached at St. Benedict's Prep in Newark, at Wagner and Rhode Island. He led UConn to back-to-back national championships in 2023 and '24, the fifth and sixth for the program.

PREFACE
By Dom Amore

On May 8, 2012, I got a call from one of my bosses at the *Hartford Courant* with an assignment. Jim Calhoun was about to turn seventy. "See if he'll sit down for an interview."

I was dubious. What big-time college coach would, on one day's notice, sit down for a lengthy interview? And about what? What *wasn't* known about the Hall of Fame coach? And then there was his legendary volatility.

But I asked, and Phil Chardis, UConn's sports information director, got back to me within an hour. "Jim says he can do it today. Can you get here?"

I hopped in my car, drove to UConn, and soon found out that there was, indeed, far more to Jim Calhoun than I—and probably most of Connecticut and the sports world—really knew. The heat of the basketball battles behind him, we talked for nearly two hours, about his interests, his philosophies on coaching, relationships, life. My favorite point: Whenever he gave a player one of his famous "quick hooks," he reminded me, he always put him back in the game quickly to say, "You see, I believe in you."

Though he was not yet ready to say it, Jim had coached his last game at UConn. He retired before the next season started, but as he looked back on the eve of turning seventy, two things seemed of utmost importance.

First, he wanted to build "a program," not just winning teams. He wanted UConn to be a place where former players could come back, knowing they had a home there.

And second, when people mentioned the elite schools in college basketball—Duke, Kentucky, Kansas, North Carolina, UCLA—he wanted them to mention UConn in that same sentence.

The first came naturally. As you will read through the chapters of this book, Jim Calhoun has many former players, many former colleagues, but no former friends. His relationships were not transactional, a concept, I would learn, that also applied to *our* relationship, which began that day.

Jim Calhoun is obsessed with, perhaps addicted to, helping people. His life story is well known. A teenager whose world was potentially shattered by the sudden loss of the father he idolized, his basketball dreams dashed by the need to earn a living to support his family, Jim is not the first to be lifted from despair by his community, his teachers, coaches, and family, and won't be the last. But not many take the obligation to give back, to pay it forward, to the extent that he has throughout his life.

Once he found his life's calling—to coach—he used the opportunity to help countless young men and women, lifting them from their circumstances, giving them the chance to see great things before them and what it would take to achieve those great things. He had Hall of Fame players on his rosters, All-Americans, high NBA draft picks. But how many college coaches can say they had a student manager, who never played, go on to become the NBA's coach of the year? These things happened because no one around him was ever too big, too talented, too small or unknown, to be offered his help, in whatever form that help would have the most impact.

I have often mused that Jim Calhoun could pick a sport he knows nothing about—soccer, field hockey, badminton—read a book on it from cover to cover, and then go out and coach a team effectively. Because he didn't coach basketball, he coached *people*, and, by the way, he has never stopped.

So Jim Calhoun built a program at UConn, a "culture," a "family." These things were not mere buzzwords to use when visiting a recruit; they were, he likes to say, "the way we did things." Happily, these tenets have survived at UConn after he retired.

The second item would take years of blood, sweat, and tears. But first, it took a vision.

UConn basketball was a nice New England program back in the day. There were successes, National Invitation Tournament (NIT) or National Collegiate Athletic Association (NCAA) appearances, big victories against teams from neighboring states. In 1976, the great Dee Rowe got them into the Sweet 16.

But when school officials accepted an invitation to join the new Big East, many wondered if Connecticut belonged in the company of teams such as Syracuse, Georgetown, Villanova. Its early years suggested it may not.

Jim was at Northeastern, his first college job, leading those Huskies to new heights. When they defeated UConn in 1985, the lightbulb clicked on: UConn and Jim Calhoun were made for each other.

From some legendary basketball minds came the advice: Don't do it, you can't win there. Jim Calhoun's response: Just watch. Even if his first practices and home games were in an old field house, shared with the track team, where coaches and players would flinch when a starting gun went off, he saw potential, saw passion in Connecticut and believed he could ignite it. To this day, he will tell you the ingredients were there at UConn—it just needed the right guy in the kitchen, stirring the pots.

Before he left that field house to play in the new Gampel Pavilion, it was packed and loud. Fire marshals had to look the other way, and dust shook down from the rafters until the players could barely see each other.

If you're unfamiliar with Connecticut, it's like this: Half the state considers itself part of the Boston sports orbit, the other half, part of the New York scene. The feeling was always that we couldn't have nice things. We couldn't keep our NHL franchise; the Patriots played us for fools. Then came Jim Calhoun. He made Connecticut *the big leagues.* And he kept it there, the quality of life always the better for it.

He began by tightening borders, making sure the best players in the state stayed home. Then he began convincing top—but undervalued—players all over the country, the world, that if Georgetown or Syracuse didn't want them, they could come to UConn and beat their dream schools. Within a few years, UConn dominated the league and became a dream destination.

You don't need to read it here to know that Jim Calhoun won three national championships at UConn. His successors, Kevin Ollie and Dan Hurley, have excelled on the foundation he left behind, and today, if UConn is not one of the "old money" elites of college basketball, it is certainly a "blue blood." No program has been more successful over the last quarter-century, and there is no end in sight.

Jim is eighty-two, has had more than his share of health problems, but he often drives from his home to the University of Saint Joseph, where he started up a Division III program in 2017, or to UConn to watch practice and, at Hurley's invitation, talk to a player or give the squad a "GOAT Talk" before its next big game.

Wherever he is, though, his phone is rarely silent. Always there are former players, former staffers, old friends, checking in, telling him they love him, and, more importantly, hearing it from him. Being "as close as the phone" is not a cliché, either, not to anyone who needs him.

And therein came the inspiration for *More than a Game*. Jim had read a book called *The Wax Pack*, in which author Brad Balukjian opened an old pack of baseball cards and traveled the country, writing about the lives of each of those players. Coach wanted to tell *his* stories, the stories of people and players who had come into his life, the relationships, how he'd helped them, how they'd helped him. Mirroring his life, this list would not be limited to just the players who scored the most points, went on to the most glamourous NBA careers, but it would also include the kid he coached at Dedham High who went on to work for NASA; the young man he recruited to Northeastern who went on to become president of a college; the Division III ballplayer who was told he shouldn't study to be a dentist but try for something easier; players who made it to the Hall of Fame with him, the greatest shooter who ever lived (in Jim's biased opinion), and players who continue to fight for the "everyday victories" that matter.

During the fifteen months Jim and I worked on this project, I, too, went through a difficult family situation. Jim, sensing I needed to talk about it, would put the project aside and offer a sympathetic ear, wise advice, and reassurance before we resumed the work. When he sees trouble, Coach runs to it; even if he doesn't get there, physically, as fast as he used to, he gets there.

So this is a story, not about basketball, not about a game, but something more than a game. It's a story about how the UConn men's basketball culture came into existence, not just by recruiting great players, winning, then going to get the next one, but by building relationships that have stood the test of time, of decades, in fact.

Jim Calhoun will never be forgotten—not in Connecticut, or in college basketball's universe. But here it is hoped he is remembered as more than a guy with a thick Boston accent, who talks fast, drifting on and off point, who worked officials hard and his players harder, demanding nothing more than the best those around him had to give, believing they always had more to give than they believed themselves.

He should be remembered not as a relentless competitor who would stop at nothing to win a game, but as a man who would drop everything and throw himself into helping someone else win their battles, whatever the stakes.

—Dom Amore
Branford, Connecticut
October 14, 2024

When I lost my dad, I had to be the man of the house for a few years. My college basketball dreams had to wait.

Credit: UConn

CHAPTER 1

The Power of Just Being There

There are only two things you are directly responsible for: your effort and your attitude.

Life is not always nice. Life is difficult, and the key thing is for people to find their importance.

For me, life became very difficult at a young age, when my dad died. I was fifteen and a half, and I had to work, become "the man of the family," help my mother with my brothers and sisters. I had to push my dreams aside and learn survival skills.

I had a difficult time, but for the people in my life—people *changed* my life. They were there for me. I don't ever remember saying to myself, "I'm going to take this on," but I took it on because that's the example my father set in our too-brief time together on Earth, and that's what others did for me when I lost him.

I want this book to be about that—about being there—because we don't always realize, whether you're a father, brother, coach, teacher, or friend, you have a place where you can help change people's lives. The older I get, the more I appreciate the opportunities to do things that are more important, more rewarding than winning games and cutting down nets, as important and rewarding as championships are. It's the opportunities the achievements gave me that matter so much to me now.

You're interacting with people all day long; whatever your job, sucky as it may be at times, you can change people's lives. I never knew I was doing it, but now, at eighty-two, I find myself overtly trying to do it. How can I get this person, this kid, to where he or she wants to be in their life? It doesn't always work, it doesn't always end perfectly, but it's important to understand the impact you can have on people. It's important to try, and it's worth it.

For me—I've told the story many times, to youngsters I recruited and in my first book, *Dare to Dream.* The worst day of my life, the worst day a fifteen-year-old playing baseball could ever imagine, turned out to be a turning point. I'll never forget the guy's steps, the words which I heard: "Hey, Jim, your dad just died. You better get home." And the walk home.

My dad was always helping people. He grew up outside of Boston, and if something happened, my dad, who had lost his father at a young age, would go. His sisters, his brother, he took care of his family and other people. My dad had a big heart, and he knew right from wrong.

I watched him as the leader of his family, and a leader in our small circle within Braintree, Massachusetts, small-town America in the 1950s. He was one of those people who was not a politician, but was there for people, and always talking to them. Great storyteller. We went to football games together every Friday night, did a lot of things together. So I had a great role model, even if it was only for fifteen and a half years. And when I lost him, I might have been lost, except for the people who stepped in.

First there was my high school coach, Fred Herget, who was very tough on me. He was a tough, tough guy. Smoked a cigar, loved going to Suffolk Downs, served in the Korean War. He had no problem kicking me in the ass. No problem at all. But he was always there for me.

Many of the players I recruited to play for me at Northeastern, at UConn, at the University of Saint Joseph, might tell you today that I was a "father figure" in their life. Some may tell you I was the figure that was missing in their life. I consider that the ultimate reward, because that was Fred Herget to me.

"You weren't very good last night. You showed up late." He'd push you. I didn't realize it at the time, how important that was for me. My football coach, Arigo LaTanzi, even though I was better at basketball, he was there. The principal of the school, he was there. I remember these guys like it was yesterday. These people wouldn't let go of me, even after I graduated from high school, if they thought I was slipping away. "I hear you're hanging around in Quincy all the time. I heard you got in a fight down there."

Fred Herget told me, "You gotta get out of here. You're going to get some girl pregnant, you're going to get married, and all that you have to give is going to get shut off." I remember the words verbatim. These people saw something more for me, and forced me to see it for myself. That's what people who understand the way they can change someone's life can do.

This is what I have tried to do my whole life, this is the "culture"—to use a word that is used a lot in sports today, particularly in college basketball—that I've tried to build and maintain and take with me, from Old Lyme High School in Connecticut in 1969, to this very day, when I arrive at my office at St. Joe's and the phone begins to ring.

It may be a former player who has become a big star in basketball, or a success in some other walk of life, or maybe a former player who is still trying to find his way. It may be one of the branches of my coaching "tree" who needs a sympathetic ear as he navigates this crazy world that college basketball has become, with name/image/likeness money being thrown around. (Let's call it what it is: buying players.)

It may be one of my former players, now a father himself, asking what I think is going on with his children. It may be one of the kids who played for me before I stopped coaching at St. Joe's, who needs a reminder to work hard at the game, or on his academics. I want to be there for them. I still consider myself their coach; that didn't change when their eligibility ran out, didn't change when I stopped coaching. (Well, actually, I've never stopped coaching; I just don't need to win any more basketball games.)

I was a quiet teenager, particularly after my dad died. I did a lot of thinking. I was pissed off at the world. You lose your idol, your leader, the guy that walked into a room and everybody looked up to. I went to his wake, but my mother didn't want me to see his casket.

So I had an edge to me. Maybe these people around me knew a little more about me than I knew about myself. There were people in my life that clearly altered my path in every way. They got me that job; they made sure I straightened out; and they made sure, once everything got straightened out in my family, that I went back to school. The bottom line was to get me going and lead the kind of life I needed to lead.

Our town, Braintree, was right on the edge of the city, but it had a town feel. If you were a Braintree basketball player, they made sure you were all right. I'd be frustrated during the summer, and Coach would say, "Come on over and play with the high school team, be the captain," because he couldn't coach in the summer.

I wasn't the most outgoing kid. I wasn't president of the class. I wasn't a politician by any stretch, but I was a kid who fell on tough days and the town took me on.

I would be working at the city dump with older guys, the kind who'd work at a city dump. We had a .22 caliber pistol to shoot the rats; I loved that. Those guys were drinking, drinking shots at noontime, and Fred Herget knew that life, getting drunk, getting into fights, maybe finding a girl. That would have happened to me if I hadn't been kind of a "star" in high school. Everybody knew me when I was a sophomore—didn't have a father, big family. That's what it was like in a town like Braintree at that time. They didn't let up on me; it took the village.

I wanted to go to college, and I had several scholarship offers from schools in New England, but family finances said it wasn't going to happen. My mom had heart problems; it took her a good year to recover after my dad died. She would have lied and said she was all right, because she wanted better things for me. But my older sister had just graduated, and my younger sister was still in school. I had to work at whatever jobs I could find, and I turned three-quarters of my pay over to my mother to help pay the bills.

One of those jobs was as a stonecutter, working with a lot of older Italian guys who'd been plying their trade all their lives. While I was cutting and shaping the stone, the marble or granite, whatever we were working with, the stone and the tools were shaping me. It was hard work, you were covered with grit when the day was done, but when it was over and you took your shower, you knew you'd put in a day's work. Not all college basketball players and future coaches have this kind of experience tucked away in their past, but I think it played a big part in making me certain things—hard, rough-hewn, sharp edges, maybe—all of which made me a successful coach.

Later on, when I coached, I might send a kid to spend a summer working a job like that somewhere in eastern Connecticut, maybe a scrapyard in Willimantic, a recycling place, somewhere a kid who had to learn how lucky he was to have a chance to play basketball could have that message cut or seared into him before earning his way back onto my team.

I didn't give up on going to college, and the people in my life kept that dream alive. Getting involved with guys from other towns, they made sure I visited some schools, and that's how I eventually went to American International College in Springfield, Massachusetts, where I met the *right* girl, Pat, who has been by my side every step of this long journey of ours. I played basketball, got my degree. I had my tryout with the Celtics eventually, but playing basketball wasn't my future.

I had passion. I knew I wanted to be a success, but I didn't know at what. I needed people to nudge me in this direction or that, and fortunately, I found someone at every turn to point the way forward.

Old Lyme was the first job I got on my own, as a head coach. They wanted me to be the freshman soccer coach, too. You learn at a place like that to coach people, not just games. Another story I've told many times, we were 1–17, and I learned how to break the press at Old Lyme.

There was a guy there named Pat Tully, he was the state trooper who lived in town, and he would sidle up to me and say, "You're making progress here, but you can't stay here. This town is not built for this."

So I went to coach at Westport High and had more success, and then, once again, Fred Herget appeared. Always there. Always looking out for me. "There's an opening in Dedham," he said. "They never win. Why don't you come up here?"

I had enthusiasm, I knew that. One of the teachers there said, "Jim, you're the only guy who can brag about a meat loaf sandwich." I remember the people at Dedham High, because they were very important at that time. They gave me a license. After a while, they thought the license was too much, because I had those kids playing basketball 365 days a year. I couldn't see anything else except my kids being good. When I got to school in the morning, I wanted to be the best social studies teacher. The best psychology teacher I could be. I wanted to get kids in the honors program. I coached football, basketball, loved every minute of it.

It was a football, hockey school. We were never good in basketball, but we went 28–1 my second year, and I coached kids who went on to do great things. I was trying to scratch my way up: Dedham High for a couple of years, then Northeastern in 1972, and then I started to realize that as unfortunate as I was at fifteen, I was also blessed. While my father could have helped me in so many ways, he wasn't there. But so many people stepped in, good people.

By the time I got to Northeastern, I'd started to understand who I was as a coach, and what you can accomplish—not by being nice, but by being yourself. Was I "hardscrabble," the word they always used? Yeah! I didn't know if I could beat you with what I had, but I was going to go as long as it took to prevail, whether it was for a job, a game, whatever the case may be. Perseverance was something I never lacked. Yes, it came with a rough side that people see; they don't always see the other side. I wanted my players to understand me, and I wanted to understand them. I wanted them to understand that two hours a day I'm going to push the living shit out of you, and the other twenty-two, I've got your back.

Most kids, you can reach. You have some who are truly selfish enough that they don't care. But I find insecurity is something that gets in the way of a lot of people, because it's the only way they can defend against somebody who has some power. So you have to be really creative and find ways to open them up. When you criticize, don't make it personal, and find some praise in there. I understood what praise could do. The people in my life, my high school coach, my dad, other people, they said good things to me and I relished it; I liked it. Most people do.

To Ray Allen: "If you're that great a player, Ray, I can't let you on this freaking court if you play defense like that. And you are a great player." Maybe that's a funny type of criticism: *I'm not going to let you keep screwing up; you're too good for that.*

So the idea, you were tough on them, yeah. If I said something, I had to follow it up. I was consistently consistent and occasionally biting, with purpose. I always kept them off-balance. We'd have a great game, say, maybe leading by 23 points, but we'd screw up a little at the end and win by 10. I'd kill them the next day. Conversely, we'd lose a tough game, played our asses off, but now I'd say, "Okay, we just did a couple of small things wrong, and we'll work on that today."

I never wanted them to think I was a piece of the furniture; I daresay no one who has ever been in a room with me ever thought that. Everybody needs someone there. When you see a talented guy, you just can't let it go. I'd be letting him down. It takes more energy for me to criticize than just root for you. I didn't coach like a fan, I coached like a *coach.*

No, I didn't call it "culture" then; I just called it "the way we do things," which is a great way to describe it. It's what we expect every day. The game, the kids, the circumstances changed, but the standards never do. At Northeastern, by the end, I knew that what we were as a team was different than most.

There is no greater joy than helping people. I was thirty when I got to Northeastern; that was young to be a head coach at the college level, but I had been schooled in how to act. Be careful. Someone is listening. Someone is always listening, watching.

The idea for them to take away is simply "He was there for me." That means a lot to me. I may not have been there all the time, but I was there when you needed me. I wasn't your coach for a day or a season, but for a lifetime. This is a journey we share. I didn't expect them to get it at the time, but it's gratifying when they get it eventually. Guys don't say three rounds into a fight, "What a great fight this is."

But after ten rounds, you realize the guy you fought was really good, helped you in many ways, was honest.

This applies to me too, as I look back at my life at age eighty-two. Because of my thirst to achieve something, I wasn't going to allow myself to be unsuccessful. I may not have been able to reflect early on, but when I got—maybe not to the top of the mountain, but pretty high—to where I wanted to be, I started to see the great thing wasn't the wins; the great thing was the kids, and the effect you had on them. Even today, when I go to a practice at UConn, the thing I miss the most is the interaction with those guys. I want to know things about them; I want to find out things about them.

So this book is not meant to be another version of my life story; it's meant to be about the lives of others, the paths I've crossed, and the people I have tried to help—and also, the ways these people have helped me find my own way. Every story is different, but the common thread is this:

Just be there.

Rip Hamilton handled everything with an ease I didn't completely understand. Eventually, I came to realize he just needed something different from me.

Credit: UConn

CHAPTER 2
Reading Rip Hamilton Right

You can't lead people you don't know.

> I came into college, I had a stable foundation. I just needed somebody to put me in the right spots when it came to basketball and teach me how to be a great player, because I wasn't a great player when I got to college, even though I was a McDonald's All-American. There was so much for me to learn. Coach has been awesome for me; he's been like a father figure—not just when I played but, more importantly, after.
>
> —Rip Hamilton

I was out near Philadelphia, watching the two best high school players in Pennsylvania that year, 1995. One of them was Kobe Bryant, and you didn't have to be much of a scout to see what there was to see there. You knew where he was going.

Gene Shue, the old NBA player from the 1950s and coach in the 1970s, was sitting next to me in the bleachers, and we were discussing the other kid. Rip Hamilton was fascinating, too. A tall player, 6-foot-6, with guard skills, but Shue thought there was a certain immaturity to his game. I liked him. Yes, there was a certain immaturity about him physically—he was 150 pounds—and you thought maybe mentally, too. He was just a kid who wanted to enjoy his life. He didn't think everything was dead serious the way I did. Rip had a way of being eternally optimistic in everything he did; I was conditioned to fight for everything.

I recruited him like crazy. I knew he could be big deal at UConn, even though I didn't quite understand him. Rip Hamilton cared, cared as much as I did, but I had to figure that out. Maybe I resented him being normal instead of being maniacal.

We hung in there with him. I worked hard; my assistant, Karl Hobbs, worked hard. We didn't know if we were going to get him. His mother, Pam, an educator, a very smart woman who wanted to be sure Rip was focused on academics, was not so sure she wanted him to go to UConn. She'd have to be convinced. His father, "Big Rip," was a truck driver, a tough man, also fascinating, and he seemed to think I was just the right kind of coach for Richard Clay Hamilton. Rip had a father in his life, a strong foundation, and he'd gotten some good, hard coaching back in Pennsylvania. He needed a coach to show him what it would take to win in college and beyond.

He came to UConn to visit, and we had him sitting across from the bench, rather than right behind us. To this day, Rip thinks that was part of the strategy, to sit him where he couldn't hear my choice of words during the game. (On this one point, he gives himself a little too much credit. I've cussed in front of presidents.)

Whatever it took, we finally got him. One of the first McDonald's All-Americans we got during my time at UConn, but, damn, they were well-chosen. Rudy Gay. Khalid El-Amin. Taliek Brown. Charlie

Villanueva. I may have misinterpreted Rip's demeanor at times, but as a player? There was no misinterpreting Rip Hamilton's game.

I'd never had a player quite like him. The only player I'd ever seen like him was John Havlicek, and that's not a comparison a Bostonian my age would ever make lightly. Never stopped running. What Rip was, was nonchalant, but he ran 100 miles an hour and he played hard. But he wasn't a killer by any stretch of the imagination, at least any stretch of my imagination.

So what made Rip tick? What did he need from me to bring it out of him? You can't convince someone of anything unless you know what's important to them, can't give the lead to someone you don't know.

Rip laughed easily, and didn't cry. I struggled with that; I was used to players showing that they needed me. Many of the players I've coached, as I describe in other chapters, came from single-parent homes, didn't have a strong male figure in their life, had had it rough, needed structure, tough love. Rip didn't have a perfect life, but he came from a well-adjusted family, and I didn't have to hold his hand every day. With some other guys, that was my place, but Rip had Big Rip. (Big Rip and me, now, we were more alike.) He needed me to coach, put him in the right spots, teach him how to be a great player.

It's kind of funny you'd say this about your two-time All-American, MVP of the Final Four, the guy who led us to our first national championship and recently had his No. 32 retired at UConn, but I appreciate Rip today more now than I did when I coached him. I don't know that there's another player I'd say that about.

His freshman year, he averaged 15.9 points, 4.3 rebounds, 2.7 assists; he was just getting started. We struggled, 18–15, 7–11 in the Big East. I remember he came to practice with this big, floppy hat and I told him, "Hey, Rip, the rain doesn't come in this building. Lose the hat.

"You're not a McDonald's All-American," I'd tell him. "You're a Coatesville All-American." At Coatesville Area High, Rip Hamilton could do whatever he wanted and it would turn out all right. He was too talented for those around him. At UConn, in the Big East, in the NCAA Tournament, he'd have to be big-time, be tough. He had to learn how to make the players around him better, not just put on an elegant individual show.

I wasn't always sure this message was getting through to him. Great kid, nice kid, never got angry, and he just seemed to shrug things off. But it *was* getting through; he was learning to play with—and off—his teammates. He still talks about that "Coatesville All-American" line, so I'd say it hit the right button.

I never questioned his heart, his soul, but just wanted to see him spit on the floor, hit somebody, see a look on his face, a scowl. And I wanted to give him that, give him what I had. I wanted him to show more that he wanted it. He didn't have to—he did. I didn't read him well enough.

See, Rip Hamilton never took a "big" shot in his life. Never knew the difference between a big shot and a little shot. Game on the line, season on the line, life on the line—they were all the same to him. Just another shot.

At the end of that season, we were in the Sweet 16 and Washington had us beat. By then, with our hopes on the line, I knew I wanted the ball in Rip's hands. I wanted to take the shot. Why? Because whether he made it or missed it, it wouldn't be because of pressure. Because pressure didn't exist for him. Rip made that buzzer-beater and won the game, his "signature moment" at UConn. (The next game, we lost to North Carolina; to this day, if you want to irritate me, remind that the NCAA put us in Greensboro to play the Tar Heels. We had knocked on the door to the Final Four again, but we didn't kick it in.)

Rip Hamilton was a killer—a smiling, quiet killer. He took off, and so did we.

We were back on campus and everyone was talking about Rip going to the NBA, two years of college and done, to join Kobe Bryant in the league. His family was divided, but he intended to go. He came through our bunker headquarters at Gampel Pavilion and stopped in every assistant coach's office to say good-bye. He saved me for last.

I laid it out for him on a series of sheets of paper on an easel board. This wasn't the time. They were saying he'd go to the Knicks, who picked 16th. They had Latrell Sprewell and Allan Houston, so he wouldn't play there. The guaranteed money where he was going to be picked wasn't then what it is today. He could be out of the league in a couple of years. "If you're a lottery selection, the team is going to protect you," I told him. "Good teams don't keep getting lottery selections. You're going to make them good."

Ah, but if he'd come back to UConn for his junior year, he could be Big East player of the year, again, he could be All-American, and he could be a national champion. He could be the Michael Jordan of UConn. He reconsidered and came back, returning to all the assistants to take back his good-byes.

In the middle of his junior year, early February, Rip got a thigh bruise and missed a game at Syracuse, which we lost, our first loss after starting 19–0. Rip listened to his body; when he was hurt, he stayed down. Then we went out to Stanford. I wanted this out-of-conference win badly, thinking it would really set us up for the tournament. I wanted Rip back on the floor.

Where we were practicing the day before, they had two courts. Rip went down, and the trainers were tending to him. I was so wired for getting ready for this game, I didn't want to hear or see anybody hurt, so I just moved the whole practice, everybody, all the gear, over to the other court and continued, just left Rip lying there on the floor. I was MFing him up and down.

Nothing seemed to affect him, no matter how hard I tried to push him out of his comfort zone. *Dammit! React, will you? I just called you a lazy mother-effer*, I'd think. Nothing. He sat out, but we won, 70–59. "We won this one," I told him, "but, man, we're not going to win the whole thing without you."

That must've been the right thing to say. He played better after that.

Another time, Rip reminds me, he got poked in the eye during practice and had a tough time seeing. I told the trainers, "Go get him a pair of goggles, get him something—I need him out there." He put on a pair of goggles and kept practicing. Whatever, Coach. Rip being Rip: He didn't react to hard coaching, he accepted it, and responded to it in his own way.

Rip's junior year was everything I envisioned for him. He'll tell you, I never lied to him and never underestimated him, just expected the best. He averaged 21.5 points, and we steamrolled through the Big East. Then he broke down that door to the Final Four, leading us to the win over Gonzaga in the Regional Final.

When we met Duke in the championship game, Rip scored 27 points and was named most outstanding player of the Final Four, but, Rip being Rip, he remembers that magical time for all his teammates did for him—Kevin Freeman, his best friend; Jake Voskuhl; Ricky Moore; all of them. You know what? Khalid El-Amin was the best thing for Rip, and Rip was the best thing for Khalid.

The ride home, where the highways and roads were lined several deep with fans all the way from the airport to campus, was one of the sweetest hours of my life, or anyone else's on that bus, including Rip Hamilton's.

Now the tables were turned. Rip didn't want to leave; he was having too much fun, didn't want to leave his teammates and friends behind. Karl Hobbs was urging him to go, as his stock could not be higher. But I sketched things out for him again: He could be a two-time champ, three-time Big East player of the year, become UConn's leading scorer.

He was getting good advice, and came to know it was time. He was going to be a lottery pick, eventually picked 7th by Washington, and as long as he stayed healthy he was going to have a long career in the league. And Rip was a two-time champ: The year we won our second championship, Rip led the Pistons to the NBA title. A three-time All-Star, if he doesn't join Ray Allen and me in Springfield soon, there'll be something wrong.

When he came back to UConn on February 24, 2024, for his number retirement, Rip said that at UConn, he learned how tough you had to be to win a championship. That's what he needed; that's what I like to think I gave him. He always says to me that I brought out that "extra gear" he needed.

As the years have gone by, our relationship has grown closer. That's what is unique about this story.

I judged Rip for being normal! He had fun. He might be the guy (he later learned not to) who'd be telling a joke on the bus after a loss. Never saw him do that, but that was my perception, and it was unfair. I didn't want him to settle for being good when he could be great. Jake Voskuhl, he'd put an elbow in your face just as soon as look at you, and he'd back it up. Very tough guy. Kevin Freeman, same way. So I judged based on my maniacal, physical approach. Rip is a great person who happened to be a great basketball player.

Now that his playing career is over, Rip is into everything. He does TV, for which, with his quick-to-smile personality, he is well suited. He's an ambassador for the NBA, and I couldn't think of a better fit for that role. And he's an entrepreneur, owns a piece of a soccer team in Mexico and a pickleball team in DC.

But more importantly, he's a husband and father, and that's what we talk about when he calls. "Coach, how was I as a seventeen-year-old?" he'll ask me, because he's father and coach for his teenage son, Richard Clay II. These are new experiences for him. Real-life things. "I coach my son, and he's not responding to the information I'm giving him," he might say. He wants to know how I raised my sons, as a father, as a coach, and as their coach.

One thing that fascinates him, to show you what a thoughtful, engaged father he is, and aspires to be, is how to manage different personalities, not only on a team but within his own family.

"Khalid El-Amin was totally different than me, Jake Voskuhl was totally different than me," he says. How did I coach them all? How do you leave basketball behind when you go home and sit at the dinner table? How do you go on with a new chapter in life, find a new niche?

Rip thinks about these things, and I do, too. So he calls, and we talk. He'll sign off with "Love you, Coach," but he's not a hugger. He's old school in that way.

Our conversations today are something I am very grateful for. I'm so glad I've gotten to know Rip as an adult, so gratified when he tells me I helped him with this or that, on the court and off.

Being there for people is more than just setting an example. Rip had his examples, he had his parents back in Coatesville. Being there, for Rip, meant figuring out what he needed and offering it. I've learned that giving one player what he needs may be more, or less, or different for another player who may come from different circumstances.

I guess Rip needed someone who was hard to please. I pride myself on reading people, understanding them, but twenty-five years later, I have to confess that I didn't quite understand Rip at the time. (Hey, even Ted Williams misread a curveball occasionally.) I always looked for more from Rip. All he gave us was a Big East player of the year, a two-time All-American, a national championship, a lottery pick, a skinny kid taking shots from everybody, and fighting through it, but somehow, I always wanted more out of him.

As I look back on it, I don't regret it. It's kind of fun this way, because now I know him, really know him. As I've watched him grow, all the things I thought he was, thought he could be, he is. He grew, and I grew by watching him. Everybody's just driven a different way, and I learned all of this with him.

One last thing about Rip Hamilton. We were on the court together at Gampel, again, the day they retired his number. ESPN's *College GameDay* came to Storrs, Connecticut, but we were surrounded by Duke guys—Jay Williams, Jay Bilas. Williams challenged Rip to make a half-court shot.

Rip was forty-six years old, hadn't played seriously in years, was just coaching his sons. He was wearing a hoodie, didn't even get to warm up. All smiles, he launched the ball from the Huskies logo and through the hoop it went. Most natural thing in the world to Rip, nothing big. He was in the moment, and he enjoyed it. Nonchalant as always.

How great was that? I just loved it.

The years and the team I coached at Dedham High, a turnaround story right out of *Hoosiers*, are still very special to me.

Credit: Dedham High School

CHAPTER 3
Dedham High Stories

Whatever you think you are, you're probably right.

John Cavolowsky

> When people want to know why I'm where I am today, I tell them I am where I am today in a big, big measure because of Jim Calhoun. Throughout my early NASA career, there were people who helped and who believed in me, but the beginning of all that was Jim Calhoun, and it's still a huge factor in my life.
>
> —John A. Cavolowsky

One by one, on November 2, 2022, my guys showed up at the new O'Connell Athletic Center at the University of Saint Joseph in West Hartford, the small school where I'd agreed to come and start up a new men's basketball program. They were naming the new gym for me, and my former players came out in force. They've always had a way of showing up for me, as I had always tried to show up for them. Emeka Okafor, Steve Pikiell, Donny Marshall, the guys from UConn one would expect.

As I sat and listened to their speeches, of course I was humbled. You like to think you had an impact on their lives, but when you hear it, it hits you in your heart.

Then John A. Cavolowsky got up to speak. He told a story I'd never heard before, which made it one of the most memorable nights of my life.

You probably haven't heard of John Cavolowsky. He didn't become a basketball star; rocket science was his game. I wanted John to speak because he was very successful, and we had met at a reunion of our championship team at Dedham High not long before that.

My time at Dedham was short, but fifty years later, I still remember so much, vividly and fondly. Occasionally I'm overwhelmed when I learn how much the things I did there matter. As Donny says, the trees remember. Two players there, coming from opposite directions—John Cavolowsky and Kenny Healy—drove this point home to me in 2022.

When I arrived at Dedham, John was one of the school's athletic stars. He was strapping at 6-foot-3, quarterback for the football team, pitcher for the baseball team, and he was one of the best basketball players on a team that had only won a couple of games the year before I got there. For the most part, these weren't kids who wanted to go on to be basketball stars, weren't NBA dreaming.

John Cavolowsky wanted to be an astronaut. I would tease him sometimes in practice: "Hey, John, did you solve the theory of relativity yet?" This was 1971, remember, two years after *Apollo 11* landed on the moon. Lots of kids wanted to be astronauts. They were heroes.

The first step for John was to get into Massachusetts Institute of Technology. I knew he wanted to get there. I knew he had the ability and the determination it would take to get there, and I was going to use whatever influence I had to get him to play for their Division III basketball team.

I had all my players go to summer basketball camps. That was part of what it was going to take to make a winning basketball team at a hockey school. I knew a lot of the Celtics from my time at their training camp a few years earlier, including Sam Jones, who ran his summer program at Stonehill College. Although I only vaguely remember it, I bragged on John Cavolowsky when I talked to Sam about my kids. You know, I'm Irish, and I've always had the gift of blarney. I apparently told Sam that John was going to MIT, even though it was the middle of summer and it would be months before he'd find out whether or not he was accepted.

But it was more than just blarney. If one of my kids wanted to go to MIT, a kid I knew had what it took, then as far as *I* was concerned, it was a done deal; it was just a matter of time before MIT knew that John Cavolowsky was going there.

Sam Jones was a really good friend of mine, and I told him about this skinny, blond kid who could jump, because I knew Sam liked kids. "That kid's got a chance," I'd tell him. I remember saying it; I remember seeking out people with the MIT basketball team to talk John up. You never know what you can do by just reaching out. He probably would have made it anyway, but he was my player, and I was going to leave nothing to chance. If there was a way I could help kick that door open for him, I was going to do it.

As John told the story half a century later, on the last day of Sam Jones's camp—where John had earned a trophy—all the campers were sitting on the ground, around the outdoor court, and Sam was addressing them.

"Sam was closing up the camp with an inspirational speech, making clear the value he saw in education," John recalled. " 'Basketball is great, but get your college education...' And then he starts talking about this kid in camp who was going to MIT, and it was inspirational to me.

This was what I wanted to do with my life. At the time I had no clue I was going to be able to make the grade at a place like MIT, but it was on my bucket list, even though we didn't call it that at the time.

"He presented me with a trophy and I went over and said, 'Sam, I'd love to go to MIT. Can you point me to the kid who's going to be going there? I'd like to talk to him, find out how he did it.' With a fatherly, straight-faced look, he said, 'Boy, I'm talking about you!'

"I was stunned. The only way he could have known that, it only could have come from Coach. I didn't believe it necessarily myself, and here is some guy, some coach, some important person in my life, telling me, indirectly through Sam Jones, 'This is going to happen,' letting me believe, letting me know that *he* believed I could do what I'd set out to do. He saw enough, saw something in me that said, 'This kid is going to do it—he has something special.' He saw that. He had to have seen that to say what he did."

John was talking with so much emotion, and in so much detail, about something that had happened more than fifty years earlier, and he was near tears. Listen, he didn't need a whole lot of help from me to achieve his academic dreams. He was brilliant. He went on to play basketball and graduate from MIT, to get a master's degree and a PhD at Cal Berkeley, and he is in his fourth decade working for, yes, NASA. Every so often I call John and ask what he's doing. Last time, he said, "This is unreal. I'm working on a flying car." And he meant it.

All he needed, that summer of 1971, was to know that someone believed in him, his coach believed in him. For that, I was there for him.

After all those many years, hearing something from 1971, I said, "John, I just didn't know—I didn't know I had that effect on you." Maybe that sounds like I was looking for a nice response, but I wasn't seeking praise. I just was absolutely shocked.

His eyes teared up again. He said, "You don't know how important you were to me. My dad wasn't really into athletics, and you were the guy who supported me. You reached out, tried to do something extra for me."

I always thought of John as a great student, an honor roll student, a three-sport athlete, a great kid who had it all together as a senior in high school. I coached him in football, too. I was an assistant. Never saw him hanging around, always studying, going to meetings, going to practice. I always thought of him as self-assured, buttoned-up. He was a wonderful, easy kid to coach.

But it wasn't important, what I thought. It was important that John believed someone truly believed in him. This was in the summer going into his senior year. He found out the following March that he was accepted at MIT, and I just gave him a little smile, a little smirk. "Of course you were" is what I probably told him. I believed he would go play basketball at MIT and have an incredible life. To him, it was simple: This guy he'd only known a year or so was helping him get into his dream school.

When I coached in high school, I just didn't want to think or hear anything except that we would be successful. In Year Two at Dedham, we were 28–1, and all of my players were going to be successful at whatever they wanted to do. John says that when I got to Dedham, I gave them "a complete change in attitude, a whole new way of looking at what it took to be successful. It wasn't a part-time thing, a nine-to-five thing, it was a lifelong commitment."

Someone told me I was a force of nature back then. If others were working 300 hours a week, I was going to work 301. That's what it took to be successful, and that's what I wanted John and all his teammates to see—what hard work meant, what the payoff could be. I was happy.

So I suppose I gave John a little nudge, even if I didn't think he needed it. It just shows you, be careful what you say, because people are listening. And are affected by it, one way or another. All I did with John was try to help a player of mine. My point being, be careful what you do and don't do for people.

Not long after John got his PhD in mechanical engineering, he joined NASA in 1989. He's had a variety of titles. Currently he is director of the transformative aeronautics concepts program. He's worked in hypersonics, Mach 15 to Mach 20 propulsion systems. He tells me he has to build teams to achieve the goals at NASA. He pulls together teams of young scientists. The flying car? He was telling me about that after his speech at Saint Joe's. Urban air mobility, electric aircraft propulsions. Air taxis. It was science fiction when John played for me, and now it's his job, his life—the life he wanted.

He may be sixty-eight, but I'm still his coach. I'm still proud of him, as proud as I was on the night, a little after we'd both moved on from Dedham, when my Northeastern team played his MIT team.

I always say you're known by the company you keep. John says his "claims to fame" are his associations with me and Neil Armstrong, who he has briefed from time to time on the latest doings at NASA. That's pretty good company, I'd say.

For John to say all he did that night, in tears, it gives you an indication of how much it meant to him. The act, for him, was that I believed in him. He did the rest.

Kenny Healy

> Where would I be if Jim Calhoun didn't come into my life? That's a question I really can't answer. I think I would have been a loner. But I can't imagine my life being any better. I wouldn't want a life without knowing someone like Jim, because you know that kind of caring is out there.
>
> —Kenny Healy

There was another young man at Dedham who became a friend of John's, even though he was from a completely different set of circumstances. That doesn't surprise me, knowing both of them.

In bedroom communities like Dedham, it was kind of a "town system": The same kids played all three sports, and they were the "in guys," their parents would coach the teams and so forth. I was an outsider, a different kind of outsider, losing my dad, growing up the way I did. I wasn't one of the "in" crowd; at least I didn't feel like I was. Whereas my father would sit very quietly in the background in centerfield when he came to watch me play—he wanted me to earn every at bat, and he wouldn't try to influence a coach—in towns like Dedham, the parents were heavily involved, maybe to a fault.

Kenny Healy was from Boston, a tough Irish kid from a rough background. He didn't have supporters at his games. His family had no dad, and his mother worked two jobs. They were homeless for a time before moving to Dedham, and he had lost his brother, at seventeen, in a car accident. All this was bottled up inside him. The more I learned about him, the more I identified, though I was still too young to think in those terms. I found something of myself in a whole different way.

I always thought, *Don't just take the kids they give you.* Because they were 2–21 the year before I got there, when recreation basketball started, I went to look for kids. I noticed Kenny Healy, who really jumped out at the gym. He was a little behind everybody in the basketball sense, but his athleticism showed. Who was this kid? Nobody knew him.

Because no one knew Kenny, or had coached him somewhere in town, he was overlooked. He ran track, he says now, because he knew he was fast enough that they would have to take him on the team. In basketball, he was on the JV team that had set some sort of record, according to the school newspaper, for consecutive losses. And he sat on the bench, knowing he was better than most of the kids playing. Folks had told me he wasn't a player, though one of the freshman coaches saw a little something in him and helped him with his jump shot.

Again: Kids listen. When I spoke to the group of basketball players at the start, I emphasized that everyone would be equal, everyone would get a chance. Kenny says now that this was something of a turning point for him. He left that day believing he would get a real chance. Kenny, who loved Bill Russell, could be tenacious on the court. That was his outlet. I thought he had potential.

One JV game against Walpole, Dedham was losing. When Kenny went in for the fourth quarter he sparked a comeback, changed the game. I went to the coaches and said, "You play him!" (My language may have been a little more colorful than that.)

Kenny Healy didn't play basketball for the cheering; he just wanted to win, and in this sense he fit in with John and all the others that I kept on the team. Kenny grew to be 6-foot-1, and I put him on the varsity. The older kids began to take notice, encouraging him. I got him a summer job in the recreation department, and he thrived, learning that he could work with kids.

In my second season, when we were 28–1, Kenny Healy started every game. I coached him hard, wanted him to win every race, every sprint on the court, and he responded to every challenge. One game, I aired him out pretty good for being tentative, not shooting.

Next game, he came out firing, making one shot after another. He had the biggest game of his life, and for the first time, his mother was in the bleachers. The other parents, who by now were more aware of Kenny, had reached out and encouraged her to come. "This is what you've been doing?" she exclaimed, after watching him lead us to victory.

Without really thinking about it, I just did what I would do for other kids. The others had parents running things; for Kenny, I did things that weren't being done at home. Like John Cav, I arranged for Kenny to go to Sam Jones's camp, where he also got a trophy. He was a really good athlete, didn't know what he had going for himself.

During his senior year, I knew Kenny wanted to go to college, and I knew he could. I made sure he had rides to college fairs, or to visit colleges. I took him to Lowell Tech, which is now UMass Lowell, for a visit, and did all I could to make sure he had financial aid in place once he was accepted. One of his teammates at Lowell was my brother, Billy. I coached against him when I went to Northeastern.

Kenny was the first from his family to go to college until his remarkable mother went to school years later, earning her degree at age seventy. He went on to become a teacher and did some coaching, most of it, ironically, at a school called St. Joseph's, which later became Lowell Catholic, and later at Chelmsford, retiring after forty-three years in Massachusetts.

He and his mother rooted for UConn once I got there, and he sent me a kind letter after we won our first championship in 1999. We didn't stay in constant touch, but not too long ago, someone forwarded a letter Kenny wrote on my behalf in 2022 for the Dedham High Hall of Fame.

> I don't like to talk about my background. It can sound tragic, but it wasn't. Everyone has stuff in their lives to overcome.
>
> I was fatherless and homeless when I was four. I grew up in Boston housing projects in Roxbury and Roslindale. My mother worked two jobs, and she was able to buy a house in Dedham at the end of eighth grade. I lost my brother Michael, my best friend, in a car accident when I was a sophomore in 1969. Coach coming to Dedham was a miracle for me. I remember the first time he spoke to us and thinking I have a chance of making the team.

> Coach helped me by finding money for me to attend the New England basketball summer camp. I don't even know how it was paid. He also personally drove me to meet with the UMass Lowell (Lowell Tech at the time) coach and financial aid office to make sure I was all set to attend the school.
>
> I could go on....He did much more for me, and he had absolutely nothing to gain to do any of that.

Kenny was being modest, of course. I did have something to gain, even if I didn't realize it at the time. It was seeing this letter, fifty-odd years later. Can you even begin to put a value on something like this? It's fate, to some degree. Everybody needs somebody at some point in their lives. Kenny's life was altered, I suppose, because I wasn't just another new coach when I went to Dedham. I didn't want to just take what the town gave me; I didn't want to continue what they were doing before.

You know the theme of this book by now: It's about being there for people, about helping, making a difference anywhere, everywhere you can. But when someone says it was a miracle that you came into their lives, that hits you. I knew I helped Kenny Healy find his way at an important time in his life, as I tried to do with all the young people I've coached or taught or befriended, but as was the case when John told his story at St. Joe's, I really didn't know the whole scope of things until I read this letter.

Fifty-some years later. It blows you away, quite frankly.

I have been blessed with a wonderful family, and it is at the center of everything I am, and do. This is one of my six grandchildren, Sam, who is now a journalism student at UConn.

Credit: Calhoun family

CHAPTER 4
Family Matters

In my life, one thing I could always do was define happiness.

Kay Calhoun, my mother, was the best waitress in the history of mankind. And she loved it. She loved helping people, meeting people, talking to people.

Kay would come home to Braintree from the Country Fair on the South Shore, take off her apron, and dump all the tips she'd earned on the kitchen table. "This big family came in. They were the best!" she'd say. She always reminded me of actress Goldie Hawn, with this happy, cheerful way about her despite all the pain she'd endured. Never lost her smile.

Her father had also died young. He was a horse trainer in New York City, where she was from, and he died when a horse kicked him in the face. Later, when she lost her husband, she had to raise all of us as a single mom. We were going to have to stick together, and she made sure we did. She had this great strength, great love for her kids, incredible empathy for people, and boundless optimism. Where we might pass someone in town and say "Look at that guy—he's a drunk," Mom would whisper, "I feel bad for him and his family." She gave me a great sense of love, and understanding; she had a way of finding good in tough situations, a very unique thing. There was a glow about her.

Coaching basketball and trying to help the kids I coached throughout their lives is a big part of the mark I hope to leave behind, and a big part of that came from the women in my life: my mother, and my four sisters; the teacher who saw me struggling in school the year after my dad died and told me, "Don't listen to anybody; you're really smart and a gifted writer."

And, of course, my wife, Pat, the tower of strength who took my hand fifty-seven years ago and has walked with me every step of this long journey, always knowing the right thing to say, the right time and the right way to say it. That's a gift. I don't think you can teach that, any more than you can teach a basketball player to be tall. It has to be part of you.

All the remarkable women in this coach's life, and a few special guys, too. My guys.

My dad was 6-foot-2, light heavyweight champ in the Merchant Marines, a smart guy, a loving dad, but he threw around compliments like they were manhole covers. If you got one, it was meaningful. Once, we won an Eastern Mass championship with my junior high school team, and when I came home, my mom said, "I'm so proud of you, honey. And I shouldn't tell you this, but I'll share a secret. When your dad came home and told me, his eyes got wet." She knew how much it would mean to me to hear that. Not that he wouldn't say "Good job, son," but that wasn't being followed up. That's how it was then. If you overpraise, then praise means nothing. I may have been spoiled with love, but I wasn't spoiled with people telling me how great I was, and that gave you a great desire to hear that your dad's eyes got wet.

A tough, quiet man with presence. Outgoing without ever being loud. Remember the movie *The Quiet Man*, with John Wayne? That was my father. He'd come home and say, "Kathleen! How many kids are home?" To my dad, if you didn't feel well, he always said you could go back to bed at three o'clock when you came home from school. (You could get Mom to hide you in a closet, however.)

They were a great couple, and when my dad died, it was really hard. Billy was five, Joan was seven, Kathleen was nine or ten, I was fifteen, Margaret was seventeen, and Rose was twenty-one. That was an awful lot to leave my mother with.

Dad took me places—to high school football games; to New York City, because he wanted his son to see it. When he died, the bitterness wouldn't leave me. That shouldn't have happened to him; it should have happened to some other guy who didn't want to live.

Kay Calhoun held us together. You know, the small Catholic church we had in town contained all her records, and it burned down. So she always made herself a few years younger than she was. It was a family joke. We used to say if we slipped up on this and gave away her secret, she'd haunt us for the rest of our lives. (So, no, I won't give her age here.)

She was maybe 5-foot-3, always thin, with a bounce in her step. When my sisters would come home with friends on a Friday night, they'd soon be talking up a storm in the living room. My mother would join them, listening to their problems, offering her voice. She loved that—the gossip, the girl talk—and she fit right in. She was youthful and full of life.

Mom was in her fifties, give or take, when we lost her. We'd go visit her in the hospital and ask, "What's that you're hiding under your pillow?" Pack of cigarettes. She had this mischievous side right to the end.

My mother taught me one thing: If you asked Dad to forgive somebody, he'd think about it. If you asked Mom, she probably already had. She could forgive her enemies (if she ever had one).

My sister Rose was the oldest and almost like a second mother. When I needed to go to the prom my junior year, she made sure I could get the tux, get the flowers, even though it meant giving up the few dollars she had earned. My next sister, Margaret, was more like my dad. She was tough. If I made nineteen baskets and someone complained about my missing the twentieth shot, you wouldn't have wanted to let Margaret hear that. You might be in trouble.

My sister Kathy, my sister Joan. All of my sisters changed my life, and after my dad died, women were my single biggest influence on an everyday basis. One reason I stayed at Northeastern for fourteen years, was never anxious to leave, was the pull I felt to stay near Boston and keep the family close by. Even when I went to UConn, not that far away, I worried about that. It was still a big deal for me.

My brother Billy was ten years younger, and I had to be a father to him when we lost our dad. I took the role seriously. As we were growing up, I watched over him, made sure he was safe in school. When he wasn't doing the right things, I let him know it, just like our father would have. Later, as he was developing into what he wanted to be and we were both young adults, I was just his older brother. It turned out pretty well. He became a prominent cardiologist in Boston, and now that he's in his seventies, we're just *brothers*. Hardly a day goes by without our talking on the phone.

We were a family, and through the hardest of times, a family sticks together, looks out for one another, helps one another. When I became a coach, this is what I wanted to create. My team, my players, once they became my players, became family to me. In our neighborhood back then, everybody had large families, and family was first. That's nothing you messed with. If Dad said we were going to eat at six p.m., that's when we ate, and it wasn't a "lord of the manor" kind of thing. It gave us a chance to sit down together as a family and talk. We always had our family time.

That's something we had at UConn. Connecticut is a small state. You may call it "culture," but it was a natural thing for me; it's the way I was raised.

And then there is this girl from Cambridge who moved to Weymouth and became friends with my sisters. Margaret introduced us, and Pat and I went out on what was supposed to be a double date. She was cute, she was smart, and boy, what a nice person.

Pat comes from a learned family. Her father was a brilliant man, an artist for the *Boston Globe*, and two of her brothers have PhDs. Her mother was gentle, a really good person. She had a way of saying "That's okay, dear," immediately making everything okay. I think Pat took a lot of that calm strength from her mom. I always thought of Pat's mom as the leader in her family. Everybody always called her when they needed something.

Like my mom, Pat is one of the strongest people I know, and she has great empathy, an important word in our life. While she's very tough, she really cares about people. It takes strength to give up things for other people, but she wouldn't think of it that way.

I talk to my former players all the time. One of them has been going through some tough times recently, and I haven't heard from him in a couple of months. I bring him up often, saying I don't know where he is or how he's doing. Pat says, "When he's ready, he'll call you." She always has a way of letting me know that what I'm doing or thinking or saying might not be wrong, but probably isn't right, either. If she really thinks I'm off base on something, she'll say nothing, let me rant. And when I finish, she'll say, "Did you ever think..." That's what smart people do. It's hard, losing a bad game, sitting outside in a car with me for two hours, and she always knew which nights to say, "It was only a 10-point game. Give it up. Let it go."

The players always loved her. My assistants loved her. They'd call her and ask her to try to get me out of there after a meeting ran five hours. She has a thing with them because she is that stable woman, a mother for kids who were away from home. Pat has that affinity without being one of those coaches' wives who's always hugging players; that's not her.

Pat's very private. If the country were at war, and she had secrets, she would die with them. To this day, when I tell a reporter something about my health or some other issue, she'll ask, "Why did you tell him that?"

Pat never complains. She never sees herself as being the main character, and yet she could be. She chooses not to be. There are coaches' wives who love the spotlight. When we went to the Final Four in 1999, Pat intentionally changed her seat so she wouldn't be seen on TV. Never wanted to be the center of attention.

We've been through triumphs together, the highest highs a coach can reach, as well as some difficult things with my health. But she always has a great way of not making things bigger than they are, never throwing words around she might regret later.

Pat has a great sense of never putting herself first. When we won our championships at UConn, she would be happy, but I think she was happier watching our grandchildren and seeing how excited they were in those moments.

You can have so much influence on people's lives just by making a phone call. I don't know if Pat realizes this, but she will always make those phone calls. And she is loved for it.

Five years after I retired from UConn, I was asked for advice to help the University of Saint Joseph, a small school in West Hartford, Connecticut. They were going coed, and wanted to start up a men's basketball program. At first I was just going to give some advice, but then things grew; before I knew it, I was talking about coaching again. I missed being around the kids, and Pat knew that. She was also worried about my health, that I might be pushing the envelope. She had every right to be concerned. I was seventy-six and had stomach cancer, was about to get a large part of my stomach removed. But she knew it was going to make me happy, so, somewhat reluctantly, she gave her blessing.

I had been out of coaching for a few years, and these were different kids, Division III players from local high schools and prep schools. I wondered if they would respond to me, or if they'd wonder who this old fossil was, hollering and screaming at them.

Before I was about to re-embark on coaching, an exhibition game in our old, small gym, Pat could see I was a little nervous. A local reporter had tried to interview her, but she wanted none of that. She walked over to me and said "You haven't forgotten a thing. Go in there and show them." Maybe that sounds like something out of a *Rocky* movie, but it was the right thing, at the right time, in the right way. All I needed to hear. We won that day, and went on to do things in our first couple of years that no start-up program anywhere could ever dream of.

I don't run from failure, but I do think about failure. Then I turn it into being much more interested in running after success than worrying about failure. Pat has always been great at nudging me in the right direction, telling me it's going to be fine.

You know, just to set something straight: One of the stupidest things you'll hear about me is that I don't like women's basketball. Nothing could be further from the truth. I like women's athletics; I like and respect what female athletes do. How could I not, with the influence the women in my life have had on me? As far as I was concerned, when UConn wins, we all win.

One thing I love is when my former players become husbands and fathers and ask me for advice when things come up in their lives.

I couldn't be more proud of our two sons, Jim and Jeff. My job was tough; theirs was tougher. It couldn't have been easy carrying the Calhoun name, especially for Jeff, our youngest. He was playing basketball at E. O. Smith High School, located on the edge of the UConn campus, when our program took off. He took a ton of crap wherever he went, but the more the crowds got on him, the better he played. They'd boo, they'd chant my name derisively, and he'd make the shot. One night at Avon High they were really all over him, and he scored 36 points. He would go on to break E. O. Smith's scoring record before he graduated.

Then Jeff played for us at UConn, navigating that difficult line between father and coach, as well as his teammates. I was always worried about being seen as giving him undue privileges, but today I look back on that and wish I had played him more. He had earned it. Unfortunately, injuries curtailed his career.

You know, I could go to Syracuse or Georgetown and if the fans gave it to me, I could give it right back. Jim and Jeff couldn't do that; they didn't have those answers. Both of them were determined to build successful lives independent of what I was doing, and both of them have.

Jim was an athlete when he was younger, but he chose a different direction. He has been a fantastic success in the sporting goods world, becoming one of the youngest CEOs in America not long after graduating from UConn. As this book was being written, he was making decisions about a merger involving millions of dollars.

Jeff started his own insurance company and still owns a piece of it. He became senior vice president of Wheel's Up, a private aviation company in New York, and works with ESPN. He also spent time helping me when I coached at St. Joe's.

While Jim and Jeff have different personalities, they're both relentlessly competitive and never lost direction. They have the same drive to be the best they can be that I like to think I had, along with their mother's empathy.

God has blessed me with many gifts, including my wonderful daughters-in-law, Jen and Amy, and six grandkids. Our family get togethers are big and bountiful, and though the times have changed, and the financial circumstances certainly have, I feel like a rich man when they all surround me, just as I did in the 1950s. In those days we had little more than each other when my mom, my sisters, my little brother, and me gathered around the table. That's what family does. They are the reason you didn't see me out and about after games, big or small, win or lose. When my job was done, my time belonged to them. My later contracts at UConn all stipulated that my family would be able to join me at any NCAA Tournament game we played.

The influence of family is threaded through all the chapters in my life, beginning with my parents and siblings, and continuing with Pat. Would I have made it without my wife? I may have had the stuff to make it, but without her, probably not. My point being, having somebody who loves you, who has empathy and is smart—well, that's a tough combination to find. Pat is my lover, my friend, and, most of all, my partner. I can always ask "What do you think?" and get an honest answer. She's the woman standing beside, as well as behind, the Coach. Pat being Pat, if she had her way, I wouldn't be telling you how incredible and amazing she is in this chapter. Sorry, hon, this is one argument I'm going to win.

Fifty-eight years and counting. All I can say is, Pat is still the most important person in my life, and there's no number two.

Khalid El-Amin persevered throughout his career and his life, and ended up fulfilling a promise to get his degree.

Credit: UConn

CHAPTER 5

Khalid El-Amin's Reckless Abandon

Nothing great has ever been accomplished without enthusiasm.

> I appreciate every second, every minute that we were together. I hope I can instill that same sense of urgency into my players that he did for me, because that's so important for life. Not being laid-back, but going after it with reckless abandon. That's how I'm most like Coach.
>
> —Khalid El-Amin

Karl Hobbs, one of my assistants, told me about him. "There's this kid who says he wants to win a national championship and wants to go someplace that will get him there." So I went out to Minneapolis and saw Khalid El-Amin play. If you looked back at the end of his games, he was great. He was Mr. Basketball out there in Minnesota, and there were those who said the best high school players ever to come out of that state were Khalid El-Amin and Kevin McHale.

Khalid was this roly-poly guy, 5-foot-10. To this day, I wonder just how he could have been as good as he was. He had *no business* being that good! Khalid just seemed to get things done, and he still does—with enthusiasm.

"He's got tricks, Coach," Hobbsy said. "He's got tricks." When he played in high school and at UConn, Hobbsy also had tricks. He played at Cambridge Rindge and Latin School, was MVP of the Massachusetts state tournament, and one of his teammates was a guy named Patrick Ewing. When Hobbsy talked about guards, I tended to listen. "I'm tellin' you, Coach, this kid is something different. This kid will win."

Khalid was something different, all right.

I got to his home, right in the city, met his mom and dad and brother. After twenty minutes, Khalid got up and said, "Coach, talk to my parents. I know what you just told me about winning, about building a great program, about playing with Rip Hamilton, but I got a game to go to," and he left!

It turned out when we met that first time, he wanted to know just one thing: Was I recruiting him to be Ricky Moore's backup? I assured him that wasn't my intention. I envisioned them on the court together. There'd be minutes for both of them. I convinced him, apparently, that I meant this, and off he went for his pickup game at the local Y. That's who Khalid was, and is. Always a good talker, but he has to do what he has to do.

So I talked to his family for an hour and a half, and a day or two later, I got a phone call. He wanted to come and visit.

An old sportswriter in Minnesota who knew him had told me Khalid El-Amin was seventeen, going on thirty. Now it got *really* different. Here's this recruit, this roly-poly kid, and he walks into our gym with some pretty good players, and they're playing pickup games. Three-quarters of the way into it, Khalid was picking the teams, telling Rip where to go. *A recruit*. A team that went to the Elite Eight the year before, and he's telling everyone what to do, where to go.

He wasn't doing it for show, either. He doesn't even remember this today. It was just who he was. There was just something about his personality. You kept looking at the body and saying "No way," and then you talked to him and knew you had a leader. When I talked to one of his teachers about this, she said, "That's our Khalid."

He never acknowledged that he was wasn't as tall as the others, or that he was chunkier. That never meant a thing to him. Khalid was always searching to be the best. For a guy that didn't really study the game, he wanted to see who he was playing against. He could tell you every high school point guard he ever played against; he lined them all up. He won a state championship with a basket and ran off the court. He didn't jump up on the scorer's table; he saved that trick for me.

So after we went home, Khalid called me up and said, "I think you can win a championship, better than the schools I'm looking at. I want to go to UConn." At this point, we hadn't won our first championship yet. We'd been close, but Khalid El-Amin believed that with him on the team, our time would come. Something about his personality. Khalid made them all believe—in him. When he made his mind up, he would find a way.

We'd had Ray Allen. Donyell Marshall. We had Rip Hamilton. We'd had stars. With Ricky Moore, we had great defense, speed and quickness. We had Kevin Freeman rebounding. Jake Voskuhl. We needed somebody to draw us all together, and Khalid, that little son of a gun, could do that. It wasn't going to be with a Knute Rockne type speech, but he had ways. He had tricks. "It felt riiiiight," Khalid says now. "I felt I was the piece they needed. I was the missing link."

There would be challenges coaching a kid this dynamic in nature, a kid who is seventeen or eighteen and *thinks* he's thirty. There always are. Khalid had ultimate confidence. Occasionally he did stupid things because he was always trying to prove he was older, bigger, better; still, he was loyal, albeit in a different sort of way.

His freshman year, we started out 13–1. Then we got to Miami in January, an easy city for a kid from Minnesota to get a little, let's say, under the weather. He relaxed, got a little too comfortable, too much sun on South Beach. He went 4 for 13, with 6 turnovers.

I rarely laid into players the way I laid into Khalid after that game. He was so confident, and even if he was seventeen going on thirty, he was still closer to seventeen as a freshman, and at that age kids always think "everything's going to be okay."

But it was not going to be okay, and I let him know that. He'd played lousy. I began instilling a sense of urgency that I thought was the missing link for him. I stayed on him, rode him, made sure he had that urgency to bounce back. Hobbsy and the other assistants were there to buffer a bit, to let Khalid know it was only one game. But I was there to let him know that *another* game like that wouldn't be acceptable. I rattled him, and he was glad I did. I had tricks, too.

Khalid could charm anyone, and he could recognize situations. He needed someone in his life he couldn't charm so easily, an authority figure who, when he said no, Khalid knew it meant no. The most important thing I ever said to Khalid El-Amin, and we still joke about it today, was "Shut the #*@! up."

He started twenty-eight of twenty-nine games as a freshman, averaging 16 points, 4.2 rebounds. He received the wake-up call and he responded. We were stopped just short of the Final Four that year, lost to North Carolina in Greensboro. (Do I need to explain how I felt, then and now, about playing North Carolina in a Regional in Greensboro? Didn't think so.) The team carried a smoldering fire in their core from that game into the off-season, galvanized during a trip overseas that summer.

The next season, with Rip and all those guys back, Khalid really took charge. The seminal moment—I don't need to call it up on

YouTube, as it's never left my mind's eye—was at Pittsburgh's Fitzgerald Field House on December 12, 1998.

The crowd was right on top of you there. The students rimmed the court, the very definition of a hostile environment. They're throwing stuff. Khalid was called every name in the book.

K Free takes the ball, Khalid asks for it, he takes it down and scores, and we win.

Then he jumps up on the scorer's table, starts screaming at the crowd as if he wants to take them all on. I pull him off the table and drag him away.

We got back to the locker room where I reminded him to be classy, to win with class. He told me, "Coach, this dingy old locker room isn't classy." He was a sophomore, had just hit a winning shot, and wanted to let those people know he was leaving town with the last laugh. And again, not for show. When he stood up there, that was who he was.

And this was the quality that convinced me, when we got to the end of close games, that I wanted Khalid to have the ball. I *knew* he would make the free throws. He had the basketball mind, and you trusted him.

Two very diverse people, an Irish Catholic from Boston and a Muslim from Minneapolis. I was the head coach, I'd always say, and Khalid would say he was "the head player."

Like most of my players, Khalid used to drop by my office in the basement of Gampel Pavilion and talk about anything that was on his mind—basketball, school, life, you name it. He'd look around at the trophies and various mementos of my career up to that point and tell me he wanted to put some more in there, really clutter the place.

"The winners are remembered," he'd say.

A few months later, Khalid El-Amin and I fulfilled the promises we had sort of made to each other. There were enough minutes for both he and Ricky, both started in the Final Four, and we beat Duke, 77–74, for our first championship.

"If I'd gone to one of the other schools, I wouldn't have won a championship," Khalid says. "We didn't care who got the notoriety, as long as we won. Those others schools had some players, but we had a complete team."

Khalid completed it. He scored the final points at the line, the one I wanted there, and he screamed "We shocked the world!" into the cameras when the buzzer sounded.

After his junior year, Khalid dropped by the office again. He had family with him—for moral support, I suppose—as he told me he planned to leave for the NBA. I had my misgivings, and I never bullshit a kid. If I thought it was time to go, I'd tell him. I heard Khalid's reasons and offered my support.

The Bulls drafted him in the second round, and he played a season there. Imagine, a guy who is built more like a sportswriter than a basketball player, and he made it to the NBA. Then he went on to play a long career overseas. He'd often come back to campus in the summers and we'd reminisce. Like all of us, Khalid has had his ups and downs. A very complex guy. I see Caron Butler, he hugs me and starts to cry. Khalid? He's not going to hug you, but it's the same feelings.

After he stopped playing, Khalid got into coaching, working at high schools around his hometown, and we'd talk more frequently. We'd talk about on-court situations and off-the-court things, communicating, building trust. When he was considering a career move, he'd ask what I thought.

He's now the head coach at Anoka-Ramsey Community College, a bit north of Minneapolis, and his son is there working with him, which is very important to him. Khalid says he's not like me; he doesn't think he could get away with some of the things I used to say and do today, and maybe he's right. But he talks about being firm, about instilling that sense of urgency in his players that I instilled in him, especially with our conversations after that game in Miami.

We've talked a lot about career paths and how to have longevity in coaching. To move up the ladder and get the kinds of jobs he will want, Khalid and I knew one thing was missing: He'd have to earn the degree he left behind at UConn in 2000. When I remind him of this, he says "Yeah, I know," or "I got it, Coach." That's the way he is—"I got it"—but you come away asking yourself, "Does he really get it?" There's always been that bravado there, and more often than not, the bravado works in his favor.

Well, turns out he was listening, in his own way, and on his own timetable. He realized he needed the degree, and got after it in 2017. He still needed a lot of credits, but he knocked 'em out with that sense of urgency and crossed the finish line in the summer of 2023. For him to go back and do it after more than twenty years! It made my summer, the day I found out that Khalid El-Amin had earned his general studies degree and would no longer have that roadblock to a coaching career. Khalid is too smart for that to happen.

I had to call and tell him I was proud of him. His mother is going to be able to frame his UConn degree in her home. He couldn't be happier, and I couldn't be more proud of him. Such a unique character. There's something about Khalid you can't define; he's so complex in so many ways. I'll tell you one thing for sure: You can't defeat him.

Will he be a successful coach? I wouldn't bet against him. The kid's still got tricks, his and, I'd like to the think, a few he picked up from me.

Dr. Keith Motley taught me a lot during troubled times in Boston in the early 1970s. He went on to break barriers and earn my undying respect and admiration.

Credit: Northeastern University

CHAPTER 6

Dr. Keith Motley: The Teacher Is Taught

Listen. You'd be surprised how much you learn.

I didn't need him to feel like he was saving my life. I needed him to understand he could be helpful in my journey in life, helping me make the right kind of decisions, to be the guy that would be there for me when I needed him. I don't think I ever asked him for anything, because I never had to. He was always there for me, to listen and to comment. I don't have to worry; he always checks on me, and that's all I needed him to do. I needed him to check on me, communicate with me, understand me—help me grow by forcing me to do the things I espoused as values and holding me accountable for them. Those are the kinds of things he has been in my life.

—Dr. J. Keith Motley

I took the job at Northeastern on September 8, 1972, just as practice was about to start. I found John Clark sitting outside my office with his suitcases. He'd been recruited by the previous staff, when they'd had an interim coach.

I said, "C'mon in. I'm your new coach," and gave him a book I wanted him to read.

John went on to become one of the best players I ever had, scored 1,617 points, was eventually inducted into the school's Varsity Club Hall of Fame. After getting his bachelor's and master's degrees, he's had a long, successful career in accounting, and still has his own firm.

He was from Pittsburgh, from The Hill, which had long been a cultural center for the Black community in the city. Having him, a natural shooter and scorer, on my team spurred me to go back there again and again to find more talent.

The following summer, I went to The Hill to see a game in the Ozanam program. I had talked to the legendary coach at John Clark's alma mater, Norm Frey, who'd told me about another young kid, maybe seventeen, who was coming up through his program at Peabody High, the equivalent of Boston Latin, an exam school for high-level students. His name was James Keith Motley. I couldn't have imagined then what this crossing of our paths would mean.

Keith was hard to miss. He was big, he was strong, he was willing. It was an inner-city game, outdoor court surrounded by the neighborhood, which makes it more fun in some ways. During the game, there was a bang, an elbow thrown. The kid who'd jumped Keith had made a bad mistake, as Keith was probably 6-foot-7, maybe 220 pounds. He flipped the kid over, just kind of threw him like he was a rag doll. That wasn't who Keith was, I soon found out. But you didn't mess with him.

This was my introduction to a young man who was going to have a profound impact on my life, as I would hope to have on his. That's the story we're telling here, about a player's impact on me. As John Clark remembers, we were tremendously valuable to each other.

So I go to see him, and this is my first impression. He gets in a fistfight, not of his doing, but you say, "Wow, tough kid." When you get to know Keith, you learn that's the kind of thing he'd avoid if he could. He couldn't this time; he said he was "bridged." It went against everything I'd discover about Keith for the next forty years.

John Clark remembers he had a strained relationship with his coach, and Keith Motley, though he was younger, got in between and helped keep things going, helped John get to college. "There wouldn't have been a John Clark if there hadn't have been a Keith Motley," John says.

I know how John feels. One of the reasons I ended up at UConn was because I had a guy like Keith Motley on my side. John Clark was the catalyst that brought me to him.

When I saw Keith that first time, summer of 1973, I just liked the way he played, liked his toughness. You had to be physical to play in Pittsburgh; maybe that's why I kept going back. When I sat down with Keith, who was in the Upward Bound program at Pitt, I appealed to his academic, off-court aspirations. He was actually the first recruit who said "Yes" to me, something you don't forget.

Keith's mother had him reading books all summer. Later Keith told me that growing up at that time, a Black kid had three pictures on his wall: Dr. Martin Luther King Jr., Jesus, and John F. Kennedy. When I came into his house with my Boston accent, it reminded him of JFK, and I had him. I must've sounded like a "lead-uh."

So Keith came to Boston, the Boston of the mid-1970s. It was a tough time. They were busing students by court order to integrate public schools, and it was not going well. Louise Day Hicks, a Boston political leader, was vitriolic in her opposition to school desegregation. Our campus, which had a lot of working-class kids from the suburban towns, was right in the neighborhood, right on the edge of trouble.

Keith was part of my first recruiting class, and it would transform the Northeastern program and, in many ways, the university. At that time, having five Black players on the team, instead of one or two, was a big deal, and there was resentment from some corners, people who thought their sons should be getting the minutes.

This was only seven years after Texas Western was the first team to start five Black players and win a championship. Keith and John had been on teams with diversity, and they made it very clear they had a presence and weren't going to be intimidated.

Some of the players actually volunteered to drive buses. The university had committed to admitting a certain percentage of Black students, and then the number was reduced. So John and Keith and some of the others were part of protests outside the president's office.

Keith was a good player, but he was a great leader. He just had such natural leadership qualities. When you meet Keith, whatever it is he has, it's still there. He was fearless, and he helped integrate us. He wasn't going to hit you with race; you never heard him call someone a racist. What he would do was explain his position.

When there were issues with other players, or in the community, Keith always had my back. You know, I was a product of the 1940s, '50s, early '60s, and I thought my players should look a certain way: clean-cut, no long hair, no facial hair. Authority figures at that time had a habit of saying "Get a haircut," but not explaining why, or listening.

One day, I stopped practice because a number of players had cornrows. Somehow, the look didn't fit my perceptions of what I thought the team's image should be. The next day, Keith came to my office with the players to explain their position. It was, as Keith says, "a back-and-forth educational process." What I learned was that the way players wanted to look, their haircuts and such, was part of their identity. I'd never really thought about that, about identity, but Keith, as he so often did, forced me to look at things a different way.

I got home and thought about it. I finally said, "Why the heck am I worried about how players wear their hair?" I had played with Black players, coached Black players, but Keith taught me the most. He made me realize where the lines were, that some of the things I might want to push hard on might be offensive to them.

The players kept their cornrows, and Keith and I became very close. We had lot of those discussions over the years. They helped me see the world a hell of a lot differently, through his eyes—a kid who grew up on The Hill in Pittsburgh, and was now living in a racially divided city and starting to do great things. "I want them to be aware of me," he would say. And he would counsel his Black teammates and fellow students to make their presence known, to explain their positions in ways that would be constructive and effective. This was one of his greatest gifts. The more you got to know Keith, the more you realized this is a different dude. He was just so far ahead of his time.

I was still his coach, however. Whenever I called him "James K," using his first name, he knew I meant business. And to this day, he's never called me "Jim." One summer, he was back home in Pittsburgh making a lot of money in the steel mills, but he had a couple of incompletes in his grade report. I called his mother, Cornelia, who was an incredible woman. She put him on a bus and sent him back to Boston to finish those courses.

Because by then, Keith Motley had already told me his dream: to become a college president. This was not something you heard very often, of course, and others might've snickered; in fact, he says now I was the only one who didn't laugh. My response: "So what're you gonna do? How are you going to get there?"

Every so often, I still needle him about how good a basketball player he might have become if he had focused all his attention on the game. He played eighty-two games for us, averaging 3.6 points and 6.0 rebounds, not that stats matter here. John Clark was a big reason we went 19–7 my first year. During Keith's four-year arc, 1973–77, we were around the .500 mark, gradually building the program, and Keith would get in a player's face and help keep everyone in line. He'd tell players, "Listen, Coach is going to be there for you," and he'd listen to them. He gave of himself to the team.

He never worried about playing time. He competed hard on the court, but he had those bigger goals in mind. Keith Motley became one of the most influential students on campus. He won the Director's Award from the African American Institute as the Most Outstanding Black Senior, and earned his BA and MA degrees.

I made sure he got to know folks in the university's hierarchy, especially Jack Curry and Phillip McCabe. They introduced him to Hugh Gloster, president of Morehouse, a historically Black college in Atlanta. One of the most iconic college presidents in the country at the time, Gloster showed Keith Motley that his dream was reachable. I knew he would get there, as there didn't seem to be anything he couldn't handle.

After he graduated, Keith was hired as an admissions counselor at Northeastern. He was working on his PhD at Boston College, but I still claimed a piece of his time, making him one of my assistants in 1978. The great Reggie Lewis thought Keith was a dean until the first day of practice, and they became very close. Because I trusted him, I knew Keith was always trying to help the players, while helping me learn how to communicate.

Even after he became Northeastern' s assistant dean of minority affairs, he continued to coach, and we'd ride around in my old Plymouth Duster to meet recruits. It came in handy to have someone in the admissions department by my side, especially in Pittsburgh. The more time we spent together, the more conversations we had, the more I learned about the world he came from, the world he saw. This was so important for me, as I spent decades on the recruiting trail, trying to relate to players who, perhaps, had been hurt by the male figures in their lives.

John Clark says I was a basketball genius, "and all geniuses need technicians and tacticians around them to help them implement their plans." I don't know about the genius part, but I sure needed Keith Motley to help me change the culture—that word again—of our program in the late 1970s.

As we were building, Keith would tell me, "You've got to look big-time, act big-time, think big-time to be big-time."

We went to five NCAA Tournaments together. In our last season, we beat UConn, and Keith predicted I was headed for Storrs. As always, he was ahead of the curve.

When I got the job, I asked Keith to come with me, but he was well on his way to reaching his goals. On July 1, 2007, Dr. J. Keith Motley became the chancellor of UMass Boston, and he asked me to speak at his inauguration. His colleagues were a little cool to the idea of having a coach speak at such an august event, but Keith insisted on having me tell his life story. That was him, taking on the school. He finally gets hired by the trustees and he raises eyebrows by saying, "I want Coach Calhoun to be one of the speakers." They laughed, but he said, "You'll see," and I spoke. It was really important to me that I represented him well. I think I was pretty good that day.

Dr. James K was the first Black chancellor of UMass Boston, one of the most diverse public universities in New England, and he emphasized inclusion, as well as capital improvements, during his tenure.

Before the days of e-mail and text messages, we exchanged long, handwritten letters to stay in touch. Dear Coach, Dear Keith. He and his family came to a lot of our big games at UConn, starting with the NIT Final in New York in 1988, which started it all for us. His mother, he says, became a huge Huskies fan out in enemy territory in Pittsburgh. And sometime during our early successes at UConn, Keith came up to me, felt the lapel of my suit jacket, and said I looked big-time, acted big-time, and now I *was* big-time. That was pretty satisfying to hear.

Through good times and bad, we've remained close. When I was inducted into the Naismith Hall of Fame in Springfield in 2005, Keith and his family were there. When we met on an elevator, I had tears in my eyes as I showed him a photo of the two of us that I planned to use in my "shrine" (display) there.

"You were the first one who said 'Yes' to me," I reminded him. Today, everybody does it, but he was the first to sign off a message or call with "Love you, Coach." He was doing that twenty years ago.

On the night the gym at Saint Joseph's was dedicated, Keith came to speak. He talked a little about me, about our relationship, about his career, but he spent most of the time addressing the college students who were there. Always a leader, always a teacher—a special, special guy. My shirt was busting open with pride. He hit it perfectly. The students, some of whom asked me if Keith was a pastor, stayed around and asked him questions afterward. They still talk about it on that campus.

But the most recent time I heard Keith Motley speak, at the worst of times, is something I will never, ever forget. In July of 2023, he found his daughter, Kayla, unresponsive in the family home. She was only twenty-seven, just beginning what was sure to be a long life of community service, and she was gone.

Keith gave the eulogy. Imagine a man having the strength and courage to stand up and speak at a time like this. Pat and I were among the five hundred or so people there, with even more attending via Zoom. I had never heard anyone give a eulogy like that, under those circumstances. So moving, so strong, so inspirational. It was a celebration of Kayla's life, and Keith talked about how grateful, how fortunate he was, thanking God for the gift of having her for twenty-seven years. And now, he said, God had called her back and she was going home. No matter what denomination you were—and I believe there were several different ones in the audience—it was inspiring, and it made sense at such a tragic moment.

You see, even then, with me at eighty-one years of age and Keith at sixty-seven, I was still learning from him, still amazed, and at that moment, quite frankly, in awe. There is so little—nothing, really—that one can do to ease the pain a father must feel after he has lost his son or daughter. But I have made a point of checking in on Keith quite often since, just to make sure he's all right—that he knows I'm still there for him. Always will be.

Dr. J. Keith Motley is unique among all of the players and people I have known and coached. From the first moment I saw him get involved in that fight in The Hill, to becoming chancellor of a university, Keith has taken me to places I'd never been before. He's taught me to look at the world differently, to understand it more fully. I had to have someone like him in my life, a friendship, a love. Like a son. Because of Keith, there have been many times when the teacher was taught.

I call Caron Butler the "Great American Success Story." He worked in Burger King as a kid, and after he became a star in the NBA, he owned a whole slew of Burger King franchises.

Credit: UConn

CHAPTER 7

Caron Butler: The Great American Success Story

Be a storyteller. We all have a story.

> I always viewed him as a father figure. People always say "Do as I say, not as I do," but students, kids, are always going to do what you do. I watched him closely, I watched him from afar, how he handled himself, how he handles himself with his loved ones, and that's inspiring. I have the same behaviors in the fabric of my family. I am what I am because of him. My mom and my grandmother did all they could; they got me to UConn, and Coach Calhoun took me to another stage, prepared me for everything, all the blessings that came after that.
>
> —Caron Butler

I had the good fortune to coach a lot of great basketball players, players who went on to play in the NBA, including thirteen lottery picks, during an eighteen-year stretch at UConn. Most of them left college early, even after only one or two years. If the information they got, and the info I collected on their behalf, indicated they would be drafted high enough, returning to UConn would not have made sense. Occasionally, as with Rip Hamilton, I talked them into staying another year if I thought it was in their best interest.

But in twenty-six years, and among all those great players, only one cried when it was time to leave. Only once did I have to, more or less, shove one of my players out of UConn and into the NBA to make millions of dollars.

That player was Caron Butler.

"I don't want to leave," he said, as we were about to walk out to announce to the Connecticut media that he would be going to the NBA Draft. And he just broke down.

"Caron," I said. "You're twenty-two years old. You're a sophomore in college. You're going to lose tons of money if you don't go."

Caron didn't want to leave because we had become his family, and he felt we had a really good chance to win the whole thing the next year, and he was right. For a moment, I started to think about that, but then I said to myself, no; he's twenty-two. He had two young children of his own, and age, even one year, matters in the NBA Draft, so timing is so important. Caron Butler at twenty-three or twenty-four might not have been drafted as high as he would be at twenty-two.

We walked out there and, Caron being Caron, he didn't hold his feelings inside. He was crying like a baby. "I came here thinking I was just going to do what I had to do to get to the next level and it would just be that simple, just a stop-through," Caron told the assembled reporters that day, April 18, 2002. "But Coach Calhoun taught me to love the game and live for the moment, because the seasons go by fast, and they really did. And now that I'm leaving, I don't want to go."

The Miami Heat took him with the 10th pick in the Draft. While he was miffed he didn't go higher, he made $1.7 million as a rookie, and went on to earn almost $85 million in base salary in a seventeen-year career in the League.

That's not too bad for a kid from Racine, Wisconsin, who was arrested fifteen times, and had already spent time in reform school before he turned fifteen. We all have a story to tell, and Caron Butler, I've always said, is "The Great American Success Story," and a unique story it is. Only he could write it. He worked at Burger King as a kid, and ended up owning half a dozen BK franchises around the country. Now he's an NBA assistant coach with the Miami Heat, on track to be a head coach one day. And he's a political activist, working to secure voting rights. Pretty damn special, right?

My connection with Caron Butler began in 1998, when I went to Racine, where he grew up. He has told his story in his book, *Tuff Juice*, and elsewhere: He was in the wrong place at the wrong time, maybe facing a long prison sentence, but a wise police sergeant, Rick Geller, believed that a load of drugs in a garage where Caron was living was not his because he saw Caron had only $11 in his pocket and burns on his hands from working at Burger King. This may have saved Caron's dreams of making it out of there as a basketball player, and soon he was making his talent known in high school and on the AAU circuit.

Much like my meeting with Donny Marshall years before, I arrived in Racine alone, in a taxi. Caron remembers I was wearing a UConn golf shirt and a pair of khakis, and I was dropped off at the Douglas Community Center, a place where someone had been shot two weeks earlier. I'd asked him where he was going to be, and when he said, "At the Community Center," I said, "Okay, I'll see you there." It wasn't an act. I didn't think he would be impressed by my walking in there. It was who I was, and I just wanted him to see who I was, see I wasn't afraid. As you know by now, I like to see kids where they hang out, in their element, and this was where Caron Butler played basketball.

"Usually coaches would visit the home, or visit you in a controlled setting," Caron says. "Jim Calhoun came to *the neighborhood*, a place where, two weeks prior, someone had literally been shot on the grounds of that community center....This gave me a stamp of approval that I needed."

I met a cop outside the community center; he recognized me, and we talked. I don't remember his name, but he said to me, "You're probably here to see the Butler kid. He's a great kid. Hangs around with the wrong people, but a great kid. The reason he's not in reform school is because we all like him."

From what he was telling me, the police there believed Caron was a good kid, and were rooting for him to make it out of that situation. It was the neighborhood, but he brought who he was as a person into that place. He always saw the good in people, and sometimes that got him in with the wrong people. (Just a small aside: According to NCAA rules, I wasn't supposed to go see him in Racine at that time, and it later cost me three days off my recruiting calendar. But for Caron Butler? Trust me; I wasn't going to find another Caron with those three days.)

So when I met him, spent a day with him in Racine, I really liked him. He had learned that by being nice to people around him, he could get through things like reform school and navigate that neighborhood. One day, as he tells it, he saw the pain he was causing his mother, saw it in her eyes as he was driven off in a police car, and he was determined to change. From the window of his room at Ethan Allen School for Boys, a juvenile detention center, he saw the basketball court and began to dream. With one more chance, he worked on his basketball skills and got himself into Maine Central Institute, where he played for two years.

Then he was ready for UConn. At 6-foot-7, Caron was brawny enough for the Big East, and there wasn't anything he couldn't do. He was certainly one of the greatest players we ever had. He had maturity beyond his years, and had a niceness about him. While he trash-talked a little—"We're winners, not chicken dinners"—I coached that out of him. He truly had a good heart, liked people, and was funny. He was smart, and loyal. Caron didn't have a dad in his life, and since I'd lost mine at fifteen, we connected on that level, and to this day when he calls me, he always says, "Hi Pops."

Caron had a unique gift, to go through an incredibly difficult life, seeing his father only a few times, his mother working from eleven at night till seven the next morning, to keep food on the table and a roof over their heads. Even so, he never wanted or expected anyone to feel sorry for him. He made up his mind that he had to turn it around. He was smart that way. Look, not everybody has bad breaks; some make bad decisions, or don't listen. I think what drove Caron was that he didn't see police, or coaches, as enemies.

People would say to me, "Here's a kid coming into the program, older than everybody else, two years of prep school, been in reform school; are you worried about how he'll affect your other players?" I wasn't, because I just knew he wouldn't be a bad influence. One thing I knew I could do in coaching, I could tell about a player. There was just something very settling about him—no phoniness.

To some degree, I'd been there. I couldn't go to college at first, had to work; I was pissed at the world and ended up in some pretty tough places. But people around me taught me, if you're in the right circumstances with the right people, it will work itself out. Everybody needs somebody.

So we went on a two-year ride together. Caron had to sit out his first three games, as the NCAA had ruled he'd accepted impermissible benefits to attend Maine Central. These temporary setbacks happened on occasion back then, and often I'd have to remind a player that it wasn't his fault, and we weren't mad at him. We went out to the Maui Invitational, and I could see that Caron, who never walked into a gym in a bad mood, was down, struggling with having to miss the games, worried that his career was off on the wrong foot. I told him, "This is going to go by so fast, and you're going to be great."

Caron was used to seeing my fiery side, the fierce competitor, the demanding coach. But I always tried to have empathy for cases like this, and it seemed to have an impact. He saw me differently after that. We had lost the first game to Dayton out there, then beat Chaminade. Caron debuted with a splash against Louisville on Day Three, scoring 20 points to lead us to victory and putting our season back on track.

"Coach gave me all the grace and all the love and the energy that I needed to move forward, and I was so grateful and so happy about that," Caron says now. "He said all the right things."

Early that season, I told Caron he needed to slim down, get in better shape, and he listened. He had always been able to get by on just his sheer talent. I wasn't going to allow him to be mediocre is how he remembers it. I held him to a high standard, because he had the talent. He dropped about 15 pounds. I held him accountable in moments within games, too. Was he going to rise to those moments? I made sure he didn't take it personally; I wanted the best for him.

If you caught him messing up, he would own up to it. At UConn, I might ask him if he'd gone to class, and he'd say "No." And I would be thinking, *Lie to me, will you please?* But Caron would never lie to you; he was just Caron. Charming, but not a con artist. Not usually. Just something about him. He could be funny, he could be lot of things, but all of them were sincere, and that's what he gave off.

One time, he did try to pull one over on me. He told me he'd attended a class when he hadn't, and another athlete at the school came into my office and said he was in class. He'd gotten someone to lie to me on his behalf. "The next person you lie to is going to fire your ass," I told him. "The next person you lie to is going to divorce you. The fact you can charm people only lasts so long, because something gets in the way: facts."

Sure, Caron could charm his way out of trouble—that's partly how he survived in Racine—but this was a different ball game. Not being in class could have made him ineligible to play. Again, he didn't see me as an enemy; he listened, and responded the right way.

Caron averaged 15.3 points, and we won twenty games the first year, although we didn't go far in the Big East Tournament and ended up in the NIT. I challenged him to get in still better shape, to be one of the best players with USA Basketball that summer, and I let him know he would have a leadership role the next season with the freshmen we had coming in. I expected him to be dominant in practice, so dominant that I'd have to leave him out of some of the drills because they were too easy for him. He checked all those boxes.

His sophomore year would be different, for Caron and for us. Ben Gordon and Emeka Okafor were incoming freshmen, with Caron and Taliek Brown. We went 27–7, won the Big East regular-season title, beat Pitt in double OT at The Garden in the tournament, and Caron played every game, 36 minutes a game, averaging 20.3 points, 7.5 rebounds, 3 assists, and 2.1 steals a game. He just did it all.

"Coach filled me with so much confidence that I felt like I was the best player in college basketball," Caron says. "He just empowered me to that space, where I said, 'I'm the best player in college basketball and we are the best team in college basketball, It felt like I could do anything."

I was hard on him till the end. On March 24, 2002, we got to the Carrier Dome in Syracuse to play Maryland in the Elite Eight game. Caron got into foul trouble and I had to sit him in the first half, which he finished with 6 points. We had 20 minutes instead of the usual 15.

I spent 19 minutes and 30 seconds cursing him out: "You worked this hard, and you can get us to the Final Four, you can get yourself to the NBA, and this is how you're playing?" He responded, scoring 26 points in the second half, and nearly carried us to the Final Four on his back, but Maryland prevailed and went on to win the championship that year. The freshmen who played on that team would lead us to the championship two years later.

I hugged him after the game. "I knew you would respond," I told him. Our ride was over. I had promised him when he first came to UConn that we would have this conversation; he wanted to go to the NBA, and I'd given him my word that when the time came, I would be truthful with him. I would tell him if it was the right time to go, from a professional and business standpoint, and I'd help get him there. I wouldn't hold him back. When we talked after his freshman year, it wasn't the time. But shortly after the Maryland game, we had the conversation again. "You've got to go," I told him. "You're going to make a lot of money. I don't want you to go, but it's time."

As we traveled around, I always made a point of introducing Caron to people who would one day help him—businessmen, political leaders. I knew he'd carry himself well, always make a great impression. He was comfortable talking to anybody, had a way of putting folks at ease and making them feel good.

Pat Riley ended up drafting Caron. You could ask any coach or teammate he ever had in the NBA and I'm confident they'd feel much the same way I do about him, experienced the same things. When he played in Washington, as he describes in his book, Caron helped to defuse a conflict between teammates before it could take a tragic turn. Contending teams always wanted his locker-room leadership, and he helped Dallas win the championship in 2011.

Caron met his future wife, Andrea, at UConn, and they've raised daughters and a son together. Since he retired as a player, he has been successful in following the inspiration of Kobe Bryant, his close friend, lost in a helicopter crash, to have a successful "second act." He's done some TV work, and in 2020 he became involved in efforts to end voter suppression, to educate disenfranchised in minority communities and encourage them to go to the polls. His aim, he said, is to "move the needle to the right side of justice." I couldn't have been prouder to hear him speak so eloquently on such important issues.

Later in 2020, Caron returned to the Heat to launch a coaching career for Pat Riley and Erik Spoelstra, and he's gotten some head coaching experience in the summer leagues. He wants to be a head coach, and I can't imagine a better leader, a better example for players to follow. He's precise, he's firm, he's honest, and he has a great message for players of this, or any, era.

A sweet and tough guy, Caron might have been the first player to say, on a consistent basis, "Love you, Coach." One of the best I've ever known, as a player, and as a person.

"I've never thought about where I'd be if Coach didn't walk into Douglas Community Center that day," Caron says now. "I'm just happy as hell he did, happy as hell my past didn't scare him off. And I'm glad he still calls me his son to this day."

You know, some people have bad things happen to them, and they blame someone else. And some people have bad things happen to them, and they become Caron Butler.

Steve Pikiell was my captain and a major locker room influence on our early teams at UConn. It's no surprise he has gone on to become a successful coach.

Credit: UConn

CHAPTER 8

Steve Pikiell: Undercover Agent for Good

Put your signature on everything you do.

> The message at our first meeting was "I don't hear the balls bouncing." That really registered with me. I wanted to make sure when he walked into the field house, he heard the ball bouncing—and it was me. Right away, he started to make me think about things differently. He toughened me up in a lot of ways.
>
> —Steve Pikiell

At least once a week, my cell phone goes off and I recognize the New Jersey area code. It's one of my guys, one of the people who played a big role in building what we built at UConn—that word "culture" again—and the conversation invariably starts this way: "Coach—how'd you do it?"

That's Steve Pikiell's opening line because, of course, he is a coach himself now, and in a changing world, he's still one of the best. He took a Stony Brook program that won only four games the year he got there and led them to the NCAA Tournament. He took Rutgers, at the bottom of the Big Ten, and made it a perennial postseason contender. Steve knows what he's doing, but it doesn't hurt to have someone to listen, and he calls to vent, to commiserate, ask for some advice, or all of the above. I'm still here for that, for him.

Steve has left his signature everywhere he has been, and that includes UConn. Even though his injuries prevented him from having the career he wanted, his signature was all over our success.

When I got hired at UConn in 1986, Steve had already committed to play for Dom Perno, whom I had replaced. He was the best high school player in the state of Connecticut, and I didn't want him going anywhere else, for any reason. The way things were then, and the way he is, he didn't have any ideas about backing out of his commitment; he could have gone anywhere, but he wanted to play for UConn.

I went out to meet him and his family. He was one of eight children, and I started calling him "America's Kid." He was one of the greatest of all time. The All-American teenager. Polite. Smart. Funny. When I visited their home, it was as close to *The Waltons* as you'd find in a blue-collar New England industrial town like Bristol, Connecticut. Wonderful folks, old-school values. *We're going to be good, we're going to work, and we're going to win* was the thought I wanted to impart clearly and forcefully, and he picked up on it. "Steve, you're going to work and you're going to win," his father told him, "and that's what you've always done."

Everybody in the family was sweet and polite. I thought, *Not only am I getting the player of the year in Connecticut, I'm getting a kid with great character.* Everything about it just felt good. You never know what you're getting when you take over at a new place; here I knew

I was getting someone who was going to help me get through the early days at UConn.

During our first meeting as a team in the fall of 1986, I told one kid to take off his hat, another to sit down and listen. I told them I'd been in the gym, the leaky old field house where we had buckets to catch the rainwater coming in, and the track team practiced at the same time, on the other side of black curtains. Try running a basketball practice when you know a starting gun could go off every few minutes. What I didn't hear was balls bouncing, and that had to change. "Are you basketball players?" I asked them. "Or are you just here to have fun?"

We went on long runs, hit the weights. I trained them hard, and Steve Pikiell, who didn't know any other way to do it, jumped right in with the others in that class, sticking close to Gerry Besselink, a great kid who had been on the team the year before. The other freshmen, Tate George and James Spradling, followed Steve's lead.

We sometimes say in life, "The squeaky wheel gets the grease." Steve Pikiell was never a squeaky wheel. He was a silent builder of character. Even after his shoulder injuries made it impossible for him to play more than a handful of minutes here and there, I made him a captain, the only two-year captain I ever had. Then he was a graduate assistant coach. The way he could talk to other players, sitting on the bench, on the buses—he was a special guy. Always seemed to know the right thing to say. When he came into your office, it wasn't to kiss your ass; it had purpose to it. It could be academic, it could be about basketball. It had humor to it, along with a purpose. You realized right away, even when he was young, that he could be a leader. He could talk to a Cliff Robinson, who was much older and would go on to play nineteen years in the NBA.

Steve was with me for six years, and it gave me a coach inside the locker room, an undercover agent—that's what I used to call him. I knew that Steve was smart enough, loyal enough to play that role in a constructive way. He was the perfect guy to help build the culture. You hear Danny Hurley use the term "secret sauce" a lot to explain the phenomenal success he's had at UConn. Well, Steve Pikiell was our secret sauce in the locker room, someone who could build bridges, facilitate relationships.

When I had my son Jeff play for me, he was great, but if I'd taken nails and pounded them through Jeff's fingernails, he still wouldn't have told me about another player, which is admirable. But Steve was someone who could go into the trenches, where I couldn't go, where the other coaches couldn't go, and take the pulse of our team. He was never going to squeal on anybody. Rather, he was a communicator, telling me what they could not, getting my messages across in ways they better understood. Steve had no vendettas, no agendas; it wasn't like "I'm going to play more if I do this or say that." Sitting and talking with other players, he helped get us through the storms, and those early years were stormy. Steve was a calming influence at a tumultuous time.

Our field house was such a mess. One day, I had all the players come in and paint the locker room rather than waiting for the red tape to be cut and the school to do it, just so we wouldn't have to look at the dirty walls anymore. Steve was right there with a brush, ready to go; he was so appreciative just to be at UConn, and it rubbed off on others. (So did a lot of the paint.)

Even as a young kid, he got it; he truly understood. I could be hard on him, and he'd take it the right way, setting another good example for the others. Whenever he's asked about me, he tells this story: We were playing up at Syracuse, one of the first games we had that could be classified as a big game. Steve started, and we lost the opening tip. I guess I thought he should have gotten the loose ball. I immediately called time and took him out, put in John Gwynn. Steve came back to the bench, asking, "What just happened?" He never went back in.

To this day, Steve asks, rhetorically, "What could I have possibly done in three seconds to get taken out of the game?" I still don't have an answer for that, and he still laughs about it, saying he still hasn't figured it out. But he will also tell you that whenever he did play after that game, especially if he started, he was diving for any loose ball, hitting the floor no matter how much pain he might have been in. That, of course, was the message I'd wanted him, and all our players, to receive. That was going to be UConn basketball from then on: Every second mattered, whether it was the opening tip or the last shot before the buzzer.

Steve led St. Paul High to conference titles, and the state championship game as a senior, and he played a lot more for us as a freshman at UConn than fans may remember, 30 minutes a game. Once he knew what "a good summer" looked like, he had a great one after his freshman year and came back in tremendous shape.

But all the while, he was grinding his shoulder up. His first or second practice, he fell hard and we knew it was separated. He kept separating, or dislocating, it. Eventually, his right shoulder became so loose it wouldn't stay in place, and if they operated to tighten it up, which they eventually did, he wouldn't have the range of motion to shoot the ball the way he grew up shooting. So he played less after that, but we won the NIT in 1988, the run that started it all, and two years later, in our "Dream Season," we won the Big East title for the first time and reached the Elite Eight. I knew Steve wanted to play more than anyone, that it killed him when he couldn't.

I don't need to quote the stats. They're meaningless. Steve was an important part of everything that was happening, regardless. Like I said, he was an undercover agent, for good. He could reach out to kids from all different backgrounds, much different from his own. Only later when I'd talk to some of those players did I truly understand how many things he was involved in. Everybody respected him. You ask the guys who were around at that time. It wasn't "the enemy within"; he had a positive influence on everything we did, helping the team every single day.

I did make sure, when a recruit came to visit in those years, that Steve was the player who'd show him around, tell him what UConn was all about, meet the parents. If I had to cancel a speaking engagement somewhere, I'd ask Steve to go. Who but the "All-American Kid" could be better suited for roles like that?

Steve talks now about the magnitude of what we accomplished, going from dead last in the Big East, which had three Final Four teams in 1985, playing in the 8–9 game every year at The Garden, to winning the League and being a No. 1 seed in the NCAA East Regional, and moving from the leaky field house into brand-new Gampel Pavilion in 1990. Those things were accomplished during my first four years, and, not coincidentally, Steve's years at UConn.

He stayed to get his degree in business, that's what he wanted to go into, and then got his master's degree. He took the captain's role seriously, took it to heart, and when he graduated in 1991, he got the UConn Club Senior Athlete Award for outstanding contributions to UConn athletics. Could not have been more deserving.

Steve was overseas in Ireland, doing some things with the national team, when I had an opening for a graduate assistant. He hadn't thought much about being a coach, he said, but he'd always be in the film room, watching with the assistants, a real student of basketball. So I told him he'd make a hell of a coach and got him to come back. That launched his coaching career.

"When I was a player, I didn't always understand the method behind his madness," Steve says. Now, as an assistant, he'd sit in the room we called "the bunker" at Gampel and he began to understand. Steve learned some of our secrets, like when I blew my stack and abruptly ended practice, threw everybody out of the gym—Howie Dickenman would yell, "Send them home, Jim; put 'em on a bus, get a limo"—we'd planned it all along, to make sure the *next* practice was better.

Steve was an assistant at Yale, at Wesleyan, and under Howie Dickenman at Central Connecticut, where he got what he calls "The Howie Experience," and then at George Washington under Karl Hobbs. You could see the evolution; he's a natural coach.

In 2005, Stony Brook hired Steve Pikiell, the first of my former players to become a Division I head coach. His first few years were tough, and then he achieved the first winning season in the school's D-I history. He started stringing together 20-win seasons, America East regular-season titles, and finally, in 2016, led his team to the conference tournament title and the automatic NCAA bid. He was ready to move on, move up.

Every move he makes, or opportunity that has come along, he calls me first. He knows that I have no agenda, just like he didn't when he played for me, except to tell Steve the truth, tell him what I think. He's considered jobs in places where, I told him, he might be at the mercy of admissions officers or administrators, or might not have enough in the way of scholarships or aid to offer, just to give him my lens to look through.

Steve could probably have stayed at Stony Brook forever, and they'd have named the gym after him. But when Rutgers came calling, I told him I thought he was ready for the immense challenge of coaching in the Big Ten. Maybe my advice isn't always right, but it's always unconditional.

He has four kids, and we talk a lot about raising children while doing a job that is always pulling you away; we might talk about investments and such, but it usually gets back around to basketball. I watch his games as often as I can. If I tell him there is something I don't like, he knows where it's coming from—the heart—and where it's intended to land—in his best interests.

In his fourth year, Steve got Rutgers into the NCAA Tournament, although it was canceled due to the COVID-19 pandemic. Then he got them back in 2021 and beat Clemson in the first round. He got them back to the Big Dance in '22. There are a few similarities between the challenge he took on at Rutgers and what I took on at UConn in 1986, starting at the bottom of a high-power conference. It doesn't happen overnight, but it's happening. When I watch Rutgers, I still get sweaty palms. I want him to win, because I know what he's put into it, I know how much he cares about the kids, know what a highly ethical person he is.

It's a new world in college basketball, a bit like the Wild West. Name/image/likeness money is there to be tossed around, and players can transfer as many times as they want without sitting. Cam Spencer, a terrific player, left Rutgers in 2023 and went to UConn, where he led the Huskies to their repeat championship. I'm sure that was hard for Steve to swallow. He'll call me to talk about the craziness that goes on today, to bounce ideas around about how to better motivate a player he has, or to convince a player to come to Rutgers. We'll talk about the best ways to manage the media, manage expectations. Steve is not one to compromise, but he's too smart and determined not to figure things out himself. He got two of the top recruits in the country, Dylan Harper and Ace Bailey, to go to Rutgers for 2024.

But as I watch Steve, now in his mid-fifties, operate in the world in which I once operated, I think about how critical he was to us in those early days at UConn. I don't know if I could have asked for a better person. Because of that, I'll always be indebted to him. He always says, "Coach, thank you," and I say, "No, thank *you.* Thank you for being a part of the program, because during our critical years, you were there."

Yes, we needed Cliff Robinson to be good, and he was. And Tate George and some others needed to be good, and they were. But Steve Pikiell left as big an imprint as anybody. We needed good soldiers, but Steve was more than that. When I look back on those six years with Steve, he was critical, he really was. Who else could get the hook three seconds after the tip-off and stick with his coach?

So when he calls and asks, "Coach, how did you do it?" my best answer is "Well, I couldn't have done it—without you."

No one played the game with more pure joy than Kemba Walker. He led us on one of the most amazing championship runs in college basketball history.

Credit: UConn

CHAPTER 9

Kemba Walker: The Joy of the Game

Win the day!

> He teaches you how to work and be a competitor. He went through a lot of health problems when I was at UConn, and after a while you're just saying, "Man, this guy is indestructible." When he's going through his toughest moments, that's when he is being the best version of himself. And you say, "Man, this guy is different—he's teaching us lessons that we don't even understand right now. When I left college, I felt that I could play for any coach in the world. He just built me that way.
>
> —Kemba Walker

I first saw Kemba Walker play in a tournament at Augusta, and then in an AAU Tournament at Seton Hall. First thing you noticed: his quickness, his power. His size wasn't a factor, or maybe it was, in that he used it to get by people. He played low, could put the ball on the floor. He was a finisher, but not a shooter. He was quick as a cat. A lot of guys are fast, a lot of guys are quick; Kemba was fast *and* quick. In that way he was unique as a basketball talent.

There was a player who had committed to us, and Dave Leitao, my assistant coach, came into my office one day and said this player wanted to go to Vegas for a weekend. I thought, *Well, okay, if he wants to go and gamble or something*, but Dave said, "No, he wants to visit Vegas," as in UNLV. And he'd already committed to us!

I was annoyed. I said, "Dave, go get your car, we're going down to Rice to see Kemba."

I told Pat I'd be home late for dinner and Dave and I drove down to Harlem to Rice High School, hoping we'd catch their practice. We got through traffic to make it just in time. I got a chance to talk to the coach, and to Kemba. Hard to believe, but Kemba had been cut from the Rice team as a freshman, but came back to make the team and become one of the greatest and most beloved players ever at Rice (which closed around the time Kemba led us to our championship in 2011). Some legendary players came from Rice, including Dean "The Dream" Meminger, who played for the Knicks in the 1970s.

I called Ben Gordon a "silent assassin." Kemba, even as competitive as he is, I called a "smiling killer." He's a welcoming person. We would have to watch that through the years, because he was just never going to say no, never going to turn his back on people.

Kemba lit up when I walked into the gym that afternoon. That's a great feeling, when you walk in to see a kid you're interested in and he seems thrilled that you showed up.

Here's how Kemba remembers it: "I am being recruited by Jim Calhoun, the legend himself. He is standing here in Harlem, New York, in this small, hot gym in New York City. Man, it was like a dream come true for me. I have to get to that school. I have to do whatever

I can to get Coach Calhoun to want me." And he said to me directly, "Coach, I want you to know, my dream school is Connecticut."

We went out to the Bronx to meet his family—his mother, his aunt and uncle, his grandmother who woke him up every day, his grandfather. Some coaches get upset when there are twenty people in the room; I was happy about it—one of the happier homes I'd ever visited. I wanted to tell them that at UConn, Kemba wouldn't be far away. They could come watch him play for us. It was an easy house to be in; there was a sense of welcoming that Kemba carries to this day. His mom is a very strong personality, his grandparents, very strong people, and Kemba was Kemba.

I told Kemba we had a really good team at UConn. While he wouldn't start right away, I reminded him he would have to work and earn everything he got if he came to play for us. I also told him—he reminds me to this day—that our gym was open twenty-four hours a day; he got the meaning of that. "Everybody else was telling me what I wanted to hear," Kemba remembers. "But Coach's approach was totally different from anybody else."

When they came up to campus, Kemba's father told me I had permission to coach his son hard; his parents were willing to trust me with their son. Kemba knew I was the right coach for him.

He never, ever lacked for self-belief. The one other kid I had like that was the late Reggie Lewis, who never started a high school game but starred for me at Northeastern and went on to become captain of the Celtics. Kemba had a lot of Reggie in him. It wasn't "I'm gonna get you, I'm going to show you," it was just a belief in himself. And the joy. Reggie Lewis, God rest his soul, was the same way. Those two, when they were in the gym, they were home.

Would I call Kemba Walker the best player I've ever coached? I don't know. I do know there couldn't be a better person to represent your program, especially when it comes to leadership; there wasn't anyone better for me in fifty years of coaching at all different levels.

I've had guys who were tremendous, guys who did magical things, and Kemba did some of those things. But I guess if you're going to make a basketball player a leader, Kemba would be a good blueprint to start with, and I wasn't alone in feeling this way about him.

Like a lot of players, what Kemba needed when he came to us from New York was discipline. Kemba played with a great AAU team that used three guards and went up and down the floor, and that certainly played to his strength. But there weren't many 2-3 zones you were going to see on the AAU circuit. The biggest thing he needed on the court was discipline, patience, and the guys we had, like A. J. Price, Jerome Dyson, gave him the idea: Be quick, be good, but be in control. That's a hard thing to do. "You'll be a hero someday," I'd tell him, "but no 'hero ball.' " That was our way of saying he wasn't going to be playing one-on-one playground-style basketball anymore.

He had a particularly rough game against Gonzaga early in his career, and I really got after him. "Like, he broke me down, and then he picked me back up," Kemba says. "I realized, he's doing this because he cares about me."

Playing mostly off the bench, Kemba averaged 8.9 points his freshman season, 2008–09. We went 31–5, 15–3 in the Big East, and reached the Final Four at Ford Field in Detroit, where we had to play Michigan State. Kemba was disappointed by that last game, the NCAA semifinal; he was 1 for 5 from the floor, 3 for 9 from the line, and we lost, 82–73. We had a really good team, but as a freshman, he helped get us there, and it was only the beginning.

Kemba started all thirty-four games his sophomore year, averaging 14.6 points, 5.1 assists per game, and the sheer joy with which he played basketball was becoming apparent for all to see. People on campus, in Connecticut and beyond, started falling in love with him.

In some ways, he was a generational player. His great calling card was his personality, a joy in playing the game, things I'll always remember. What he did, Kemba let you in, teammates, students, reporters.

Everyone walked away from him saying "What a kid!" And he was. You didn't walk by Kemba and say "How you doing?" and he'd just walk by. Wasn't going to happen. He let you in.

Anytime I would get mad at him, I'd feel guilty about it. Then I'd say to myself, *What the hell am I feeling guilty about? That's my job!* But when someone gives you so much—he was one of the few people who'd make even me feel that way. He was just such a good person, to me, staff, teammates. If a reporter came up and wanted to do a story, he wasn't going to give wiseass answers, make them feel like they were taking up his time.

Of course, when we talk about Kemba Walker, it culminates with his junior year at UConn, 2010–11, the year he carried us, practically willed us, to our third national championship. It had been seven years since our last title, and UConn was the underdog all over again, a young team, a lot of freshmen, not a lot of experience around Kemba.

The precursor for all that came during March Madness, with the Maui Invitational in November. He'd warmed up for the season with a 42-point eruption against Vermont, then when we got to Hawaii, he scored 31 points, 29 in the second half, in our win over Wichita State; then he scored 30 points, going 10-for-19, as we knocked off Michigan State—sweet redemption for Kemba. In the final of the tournament, he scored 29, with 6 assists, as we beat Kentucky.

What he did at Maui—those three games, against Michigan State, Kentucky, and a very good Wichita State team, big-name players, high school All-Americans—he was The Guy in that tournament, the guy who won it for us. I knew then, if he could dominate those teams, he was going to have a pretty special year.

We struggled during conference play, going 9–9. The rugged, original Big East, which had eleven teams make the NCAA Tournament that year, could do that to you. But Kemba hit a number of notable shots to lift us to wins, averaging 23.5 points per game.

Usually, late in the season, you don't run practices as hard; you're trying to freshen your team up. But after we lost to Notre Dame in the last regular-season game, I ran a particularly hard session. Kemba still remembers it. He might even still be sore from it.

"We were going back to the drawing board, and we had two 'Coach Calhoun' intense practices," Kemba says. "Roll the ball out there, dive on the floor, hit somebody. And after that? *It was on.*"

I knew they had grit in them, but it had to come out now, because when we got to New York for the Big East Tournament, our conference record had left us with the toughest assignment imaginable. We'd have to win five games in five days. In the quarterfinals, we had to beat Pittsburgh, the regular-season champ. Maybe you remember this? Tie game, last possession, and it was like the play was designed. Kemba got the ball, he stepped this way and that, got the kid guarding him to slip as he stepped back, and it was Kemba for the win. Right there in New York, at The Garden, not far from Rice.

"Cardiac Kemba" they called him after that. He did that a lot of times. Without being a bragger, he had a sense of greatness, a sense of drama, and he loved every second of it. I said to George Blaney, "We're going to win it." The Big East? No, the national championship.

After the five wins in five days, all the inexperience on our team disappeared. Everything we did worked perfectly because we had a great leader, who had this incredible ability to want to win as much as any kid I've ever met. The feeling just came to us, and I knew we could get the whole thing. I didn't have to yell at them much that month; after every win, the guys heard someone say, "Well, they're going to lose the next one." They were self-motivated.

Kemba didn't lead with a sledgehammer; he simply said, "Just follow me." He didn't say that literally, but that was the message. He helped Jeremy Lamb, he helped Shabazz Napier, he helped all of us. When your best player is your best person and they follow him? Pretty tough to beat. We beat Syracuse and Louisville to win the Big East.

On to the NCAA Tournament we went, and Kemba led us in scoring in each of the six games, including 16 points in the national championship game, in which we beat Butler. What can you say? Pretty close to a once-in-a-lifetime player.

At this time in my life, nearing seventy, starting to think about retiring, it just made me feel good about coaching. It just reassured me that being a team, caring about each other, having great leadership, having guys take their roles seriously—all of it could still happen, even if the world of college basketball was changing right before our eyes. Kemba rejuvenated me, gave me the idea that it all still worked, that if they know you care about them, you can still coach them hard. If they believe, you can still really push them and they'll recognize what you're doing. We didn't quit. The kids didn't quit.

When Kemba received the Bob Cousy Award for the nation's top point guard, he turned to me and said "Thanks, Coach." And he started saying "Love ya, Coach," instead of good-bye.

"To this day, I'd run through a brick wall for that guy," Kemba says. "I still feel that way."

After we cut down the nets, Kemba threw his arms around me and we hugged for a good long time. Kemba was crying. He didn't want to go, but we both knew it was time for him to move on. Kemba was ready to go on to the NBA, and he was picked 9th overall by Charlotte. He was an All-Star there again and again; he liked his coaches and loved the fans there, and they loved him, but the losing really wore on him. Despite the smile, the personality, he also was a great competitor. He wasn't there, I'd kid him, just to be a pretty face with a happy smile. Kemba wanted to win.

I remember one year, Tom "Satch" Sanders, who I had known for decades, and had founded the League's Rookie Transition Program, called me up and said, "We've got to get Kemba to start the All-Star Game. We want him to be the role model of what we want an NBA player to be." You can get a lot of tributes, but when a guy like Satch

Sanders considers you the shining example of what they want to represent what a pro player could be, and should be, that's a pretty high tribute. All I know is, my chest was out pretty far that day.

When Kemba became a free agent, I really thought the decision could be a defining one for him. Land with the right team, win a championship or two to go along with what he did for us, and Kemba would go to the Hall of Fame. But that knee of his got in the way, and he never really showed the true Kemba. Still, he left an impression everywhere he went. He played for the Knicks and the Mavericks, and a year in Monaco; then he decided in the summer of 2024 that he couldn't play any longer. He'd run himself into the ground. A guy built around incredible quickness and speed and jumping ability, he just couldn't do the things he wanted to do anymore.

I looked it up: Kemba made $198 million playing basketball. But he didn't play for money, and he showed the maturity to stop playing when he did, rather than hang on, even though he probably could have made some more money. If Kemba had had his way, he probably would have played until that leg fell off, but he knew it was time to stop.

He's not the kind of guy that calls me every week, and when we talk today, it's less basketball, more life. He's engaged to be married, and he knows I'm here when he wants advice. You don't need reassurance from Kemba, and that's a great thing to say about someone. He never changed; the money, the lifestyle, none of it wiped the joy, the smile, from his eyes and his face. The saying *Win the day* has been associated with me for a long time. Kemba Walker? He wins every day.

When he retired as a player he had the opportunity to go back to Charlotte and work as a coach, and he took the job the day he announced his retirement. "Player Enhancement Coach" is his title, and I can't imagine anyone better suited for that job description, to work in development. He will make guys better.

I think he'll do it differently. You've got to find a way to let players know you're there for them; a player has to know you have their back and where you fit in his life. In the NBA, you're not going to be yelling at a twenty-nine, thirty-year-old man, but Kemba wants to be good, he wants to win. He knows how to play, he has a good feel for the game, instinctively knows how to play basketball. And he's got something not many of us have: He's instantly likable. Those young players are going to love being around him.

Kemba's going to make an impact now that he's into coaching. He doesn't have to go to a book, or take a class, to reach people. Kemba just has a way of opening himself up, not telling you about his background or who he is or how great he is, nothing like that, but he's a warm, welcoming person. His smile has a lot to do with it. His joy for basketball has a lot to do with it. I'd tell him, you be you. And trust me—that will be more than good enough.

Sam Majek wanted to become a dentist but was advised to go for something that wasn't so hard.
My advice? Go be a dentist.

Credit: University of Saint Joseph

CHAPTER 10

Sam Majek: The Old-Fashioned Kid at St. Joe's

Time and effort are the most valuable items you have.

Coach always stresses that he does it for the kids. Sometimes it's hard to see that picture when he's yelling at you, but he really does do it for you, and he really does have your back, no matter what. He doesn't expect you to be perfect, just to give your best effort. He's always that beacon I can feel on my shoulder if I feel like being lazy. I imagine what he'd say. When people ask me, "Where do you get the energy or the motivation to get up at five a.m. and study?" I say, "It's easy—because I'm afraid of getting yelled at by Coach."

—Sam Majek

When I arrived at the University of Saint Joseph in 2017, Glen Miller, my associate head coach and eventual successor, and I traveled through the back roads to high schools and prep schools in New England to find players. We were starting up a Division III program at a small school in West Hartford, previously an all-female school that was about to go coed. I had coached high school and college basketball from 1969 until 2012, and knew what it felt like to reach the top of the college basketball world. But after five years in retirement, just doing a little work in TV and few other things, it was obvious what I missed the most.

The kids.

Working with young people, helping to make them better, at basketball or anything else they wanted to do, was still in my blood. I didn't need more money, didn't need more attention; I just wanted to teach and coach again. So when I was asked for advice in starting up a program at St. Joe's, I was soon talked into—or maybe I talked myself into—a comeback. I had a few health problems I was dealing with, but the chance to be there for young people with dreams pulled me back in, and they didn't have to be NBA dreams anymore. Coaching was about to become fun for me, all over again.

Glen and I were looking for players who would embrace the task of building something, not from the bottom but from nothing, to take a chance on something new. Even for me, this was a new experience, but Glen, who had been a highly successful coach at this level, helped identify players who would fit our plan.

One of the places I liked to go was Woodstock Academy, one town over from my home in Pomfret, an old Connecticut prep program that always had players. That's where Sam Majek first caught my eye. He played in some of their "A" games, some of their "B" games.

Now, when I say I was looking for players, I was really looking for *people.* I wasn't expecting Division I talent to come play for me, wasn't looking for future NBA stars. But some things in my evaluations didn't change. I've always liked to go to games to watch players check in and out, their body language, their behavior.

With Sam, there was some vibrance about him all the time. Exuberance. He was a tough kid, 6-foot-6 and 225 pounds, and he could really jump. Very powerful kid. I found out later he could hit a golf ball 300 yards. I knew he could be a player who could help us win games, but I saw something unique, very unique in Sam Majek. He had graduated from Woodstock in 2017, and was back as a postgrad when I met him. He had seen on the news the day before that I was coming out of "retirement" to build this program at St. Joe's, and now here I was at his game.

Afterward, I went up to talk to him, told him what I had in mind for the new program, that I thought he could fit in with it. I didn't realize it yet, but my pitch landed on target. He wanted to play for me, fell in love with basketball watching Kemba Walker and our 2011 championship team at UConn, and his father—a hardworking guy who had played some basketball but had a bad back—*really* wanted him to play for me. His mother is an educator. His brother is a pilot. They lived in Brooklyn—not Brooklyn, New York, but a small town in the northeast corner of Connecticut, not far from me, not far from Woodstock Academy.

When I asked him what he wanted to do, Sam told me he wanted to be a dentist. Really? Why? Because he'd enjoyed going to the dentist as a kid. Right there, you knew he was cut a little different. How many kids go to the dentist without a fight? Although he was a good student, teachers had been telling him he didn't quite have the grades to go to medical school or dental school, so maybe he should focus on something else, something less challenging academically.

I like to think I'm a little different, too. Sam Majek wanted to be a dentist? If he came to St. Joe's, I was going to encourage him, push him, to reach his goals. And he started to believe he could not be denied. No exaggeration, this kid studied six hours a day. His roommates—Ryan O'Neill, who got a 1400 on his SAT, Ivy League, and

Jake Sullivan, about the same—would tell me, "You wouldn't believe how this guy studies."

I wasn't going to get Sam into the gym as much as the other players. He wasn't going to be in there two hours a night, getting shots up. That wasn't who he was; it didn't line up with his aspirations. But his aspirations became my aspirations for him. Sam says I was one of the first people to take his dream of becoming a dentist seriously. "You work hard in life," I told him, "you do the right things, you can achieve what you want." You never know how much simple words like that can mean for someone that age. That's why I do this, and why I've never stopped.

"It definitely changed my outlook," Sam says today. "When I got to St. Joe's, I was scared to even try the hard science classes. I was even going to change my major, try a different career. But Coach was always checking in, asking how class was going, are you reading? Are you in the right spot? I didn't want to disappoint him. He made me be responsible and accountable. 'If you want to do it, there are no shortcuts.' He believed in me, and that really made a difference."

Sam came to the University of Saint Joseph, and after a rocky start, became a straight-A student and an important member of our team, which, by the way, did accomplish special things in those first seasons as a start-up.

That first year, nearly every member of our team was a freshman, and we had to go up against established programs. In our first scrimmage, Sam got the ball stolen from him and they got an easy basket. "Sam, if you want to play for the other team, put their jersey on," I told him. Like a lot of players, he wondered for a second just what he'd gotten himself into when he'd agreed to play for me. But he didn't take things personally; he got right back to work at getting better. He came off the bench, we'd play him a little more each game, and he started scoring a little more. On February 16, 2019, he scored

20 points in our win over Regis that clinched a spot in the Great Northeast playoffs.

If every team could have someone like him.... I can't even imagine someone not liking Sam Majek. He had this natural gift. He'd come into the gym with a ton of energy—maybe I'm not feeling well, or in a bad mood because we hadn't played well, and he'd tell one of his stupid jokes. "Hey, Sam, shut the #*@! up, we're trying to get some basketball done here!" And he'd laugh. Instead of being pissed, he got it. He'd fail to position himself properly to get a rebound and I'd say, "Uh, Sam, Emeka Okafor only made a hundred million by boxing out. I know you're better than Emeka, so don't box out, see how that works for you."

Sam would accept my coaching, and anything that was free. If I had a pile of shirts or jackets, Sam would say, "Gee, what are you going to do with them?" That was his setup. "What size are you?" And he'd take one. But anything you asked him to do, he'd do.

When we'd go on those four-hour bus rides, part of playing D-III basketball in New England, you couldn't have invented it. Sam would come on the bus, everyone trying to doze off, dreading the hours ahead, and he'd sound like a game-show host. "How's everybody doing today?" At just the right moment, he'd be making jokes after we'd won a game, talking to his teammates, saying just the right things if we'd lost. It was great, at that stage of my life and career, to meet an old-fashioned kid. That's what Sam is. He's John Cavolowsky thirty-five years later. It was kind of nice, finding a 1950s, 1960s kid in 2020. Kind of where I started as a coach.

In the locker room, if stuff was happening, if we had a problem with a player, Sam would be watching, looking for his opportunity to make a positive contribution. We had kids from a wide variety of places, prep schools, inner-city technical schools, and Sam, in the locker room, in the weight room, on the bus or in my office, helped bring everyone together. Once, I told our leading scorer, after a long bus ride to Maine, "Oh, by the way, because you were late for the bus today, your ass is not playing." And Sam walked by me later and said, "That was good, Coach." He let me know that he felt good about it. He had a unique way of being an important part of the team without being a politician. Not a phony bone in his body.

Not that anyone ever tried to find out, but he's probably not a great guy to mess with. Nobody was going to back him down physically. He just had a comfort level. Everybody's got to know their role, right? Squirrels don't swim and sharks don't climb trees. Sam knew who he was, and it allowed him to become what he became. Nobody told him to study six hours a night. He did it. Time and effort are our most valuable possessions, and Sam chooses to spend his wisely. He had great drive, was relentless in his pursuit of the goals he had for himself. It was an adjustment for me after so many years of coaching kids whose priority was basketball, who you often had to prod to pay more attention to academics. I had to accept who Sam was. But on the other hand, he worked very hard, and I made sure to recognize what he did, all the time. My old practice held true: Two hours a day, I'm going to kick your ass; the other twenty-two, I've got your ass.

Sam filled up his twenty-four hours a day. It was hard to get him to come play in the summer league games because he was working, or studying. But people can help your program in so many different ways, which I was learning all over again with Sam Majek in our new program.

After he did poorly on his first couple of exams, we had a talk. Nothing big. I didn't know what to tell someone studying medicine or dentistry; I just told him, "Well, if it's not working, you have to try something different. Step it up. Work harder. Work smarter." He figured it out quickly, started getting As, and never looked back academically. The basketball helped give him structure; he had no time to procrastinate.

In his second season, Sam didn't get on the court quite as much. We had a better team, won twenty-five games in a row, took the GNAC title, and played in the NCAA Tournament. Our season ended just before the pandemic hit. We played only five games the next season, and Sam played in just a handful after I stepped aside early in the 2021–22 season.

Sam, a biology major, kept right on with his studies. He'd be talking about cutting things open and working with skeletons, and joke that he just wanted to work on the teeth. When he'd report an academic challenge to me, I'd say, "Sam, I'm not worried about you. I know you'll do what you need to do." And I wasn't worried. Like John Cav, if Sam wanted to do something, I'd learned by then, you *didn't* have to worry about it. He was going to be successful.

We found a lot of good players for St. Joe's. After I stepped aside as coach, Glen Miller kept right on winning, even had the program ranked No. 1 in the country for a while in 2022. He kept looking for the kind of people that would help us do it.

I didn't really talk to the St. Joe's kids about my background. Then, after we won the GNAC, I had the entire team over to my home in Pomfret. I took them down to the basement where I keep all the trophies and such. "Walk around, take a look," I told them. I let them try on the watches from the Big East championships, the rings. Touch the trophies.

Then I told them I didn't bring them down there to brag or show them all I have. "I brought you here to tell you that when I was fifteen, my dad died. My life was changed forever. I had to go to work to support my family. It was because of my coaches that I was able to get out of my situation and make this life for myself and my family. I'm here to show you it's possible. I did it."

I was no different than them. They just had to do it themselves. It's as simple as this: I may be in my eighties, but I'm passing on what was passed on to me by the people in my life, my family, my coaches.

Sam still talks about that day in my basement. It touched him. As he was nearing graduation from St. Joe's, double-majoring in biology and chemistry, he started applying to dental schools. He got accepted to a couple of places, and then, on December 1, 2021, he got the e-mail from UConn, his dream school. He called me to tell me.

"I knew you could do it," I told him again. "I wasn't worried about you. I knew you put in the work."

He's in his second year now, well on his way to becoming a dentist, and he wants to do it in Connecticut, maybe focus on pediatrics. I bet he'll make kids love going to the dentist.

In November 2022, they named the gym at St. Joe's after me, and players from nearly all the places I've coached came by. It meant so much to me to see Sam there among the other original "Blue Jays." I talk to Sam all the time, still checking in as he enters the next stretch of his studies, and if I'm not using my tickets to a UConn basketball or football game, well, if they're free, Sam Majek will take 'em.

Listen, I've had some kids do some special things. Sign million-dollar contracts, win championships in the NBA, become great coaches, go to the Hall of Fame. I've got plenty of guys to brag about. But I brag about Sam because it's remarkable, what he has done. It wasn't just being smart; it took real effort, self-admitted effort, and now he's on his way to where he wants to be. You have a kid score 40 points after you work with him, that's great. What Sam is doing is not only great, it's long-lasting. It's what time and effort, well spent, looks like.

Joe McGinn was such an inspiration to our 1999 championship team, and an inspiration for me to this day to live life to the fullest.

Credit: McGinn family

CHAPTER 11

You Think You've Got It Tough?: The Joe McGinn Story

You don't count the days; you make the days count.

> He's loyal and he's kind and he's humble. There's a shield up, and you've got to dig deep to get through those layers, but man, when you get there, there's a whole, beautiful person inside there. He makes you want to be better. At the end of the day, you just want him to be proud. That's what his players wanted, that's what my brother, Joe, wanted. You just want him to be proud of you. I feel Joe got so many extra years because of his relationship with Jim.
>
> —Pat Thomson, Joe McGinn's sister

Steve Pikiell, a junior or senior at the time, came into my office one day and told me about this friend of his back in Bristol, a senior at Bristol Eastern High School. The kid had been very sick since he was a child. He and Steve had been friends since grammar school.

He wanted to go to college, but he had just missed so much class time in high school.

"Coach, can you help him out?" Steve asked me.

So he brought his friend to a game and down to the locker room afterward, and that's how I met Joe McGinn, a piece of work even then. He told me his life story. Joe being Joe, he had no problem telling you how he felt. A hot shit, he'd say things a kid his age would never say. It was impossible not to like him. He became part of us.

Joe's story is a story of hope, a story of finding something positive, of finding a reason to fight. Our basketball team became his reason. And he became a part of our reason because—I know it's a funny way to put it, but Joe was a walking advertisement for how good *we've* got it. And when it meant the most, he would let us know that in a way only Joe McGinn could.

Joe had kidney disease, diagnosed when he was a small child, which meant he stopped growing. He received a kidney transplant at age sixteen, and Steve brought him in to meet me just as our program was beginning to take off. He was 5-foot-2, about 120 pounds, red hair. In middle school, he used to hand in his assignments signed "Michael Jordan" and got called to the principal's office. Piece of work. His dreams of playing basketball couldn't come true, but he became captain of the golf team at Bristol Eastern and won a few local junior tournaments.

All the while, his kidney disease was worsening. I implored him to listen to doctors' instructions, take his medicine, and I would help him get into college. He went to Northeastern, and after a couple of years, with good grades, I kept my promise to help him transfer to UConn, where he became a student assistant for us. That's all he'd wanted, to be one of the Huskies, and it became all I'd wanted for him. I tried to treat him like I would anyone else, within reason, expecting him to do his tasks, holding him accountable, and his family told me he appreciated that. What he wanted most was normalcy, wanted to feel like one of the team. So I'd get on him if he forgot someone's shoes, for example. Once, I told him if he didn't get the basketballs out on time, I'd make him do a lap. He was a little late and I made him do a lap around center court. The team went crazy, and Joe did, too. He loved it. He was one of the guys.

If a player ever needed anything, Joe would do it, if he could. If a player was injured, Joe would check in with him every day, or stay with him and push him through his rehab. Like a great teammate, the team was all he cared about. He'd be in "The Bunker," listening in on our staff meetings. If Joe were sitting in my office for a bull session with the staff, he'd be right in the middle of the conversation. If we were talking about a player, he would have no problem saying, "If he'd work, Coach—if he'd stay here and get some shooting in, he'd do all right." He would say something like that in a good way. He'd tell somebody, "Shut up until you're playing better." That would be Joe. He didn't want to just hang around; he wanted to be part of the team, feel like he was contributing something. And he was.

The medication he had to take was creating terrible side effects. As a senior, he got out of his hospital bed after another major surgery and made it to Gampel Pavilion for the Senior Night ceremonies.

After getting his degree from UConn in 1995 and getting a job in graphics at ESPN, Joe stayed around the program. He could be critical without being mean, and the kids all loved him, even with his ball-busting, even with me and the staff. He was loved. He made you forget he was in a wheelchair because he was always saying something.

Joe had a fiery personality. You could tell he was always in the midst of a fight to live. His parents were told when he was three that he might not make it to age six, but he was determined to make it a helluva lot longer. That tells you about his will. Still, he dreaded the idea that he might have to have another transplant. He also didn't want to have his legs removed, which the doctors had told him would be necessary for his circulation, to stay alive.

His family was convinced I could get through to Joe when they couldn't, so they asked me to go talk to him. It was one of the hardest things I've ever had to do. How do you tell this kid, who was about twenty-five by this point, who wanted so much to participate in life, that he would have to agree to have both his legs amputated?

I started out by saying, "Joe, we need you. We need you to be here, and what they're telling me is, you might not be here unless you do this." To get him to smile, I said, "Look—you weren't very fast anyways. This is going to slow you down, but it's not going to slow that mouth and mind of yours down. It's not going to slow your enthusiasm down—not going to slow down what you bring to the team."

Joe cried. I cried. But he had the operation. Although he was in a wheelchair for the last year of his life, he remained an integral part of our program. He'd come to games, practices. I'd call him and we'd talk, the way I still do with a lot of players. We'd talk about recruits, he'd tell me what he was seeing, ask me what I thought. Hey, sometimes we'd just gossip. We both enjoyed a good story.

In the spring of 1998, after losing his legs, Joe was haranguing Rip Hamilton, in his way, for even *thinking* about going to the NBA. Rip stayed at UConn, and Joe put in for vacation time a year in advance so he'd be able to go to the Final Four. The joy he got out of life was the team, and our opponents became his enemies. Being happy with a win, pissed after a loss, gave him other things to think about when he was sick, when he was depressed about his condition. He didn't have to fight his illness; he could fight the SOBs on the other teams.

In March of 1999, as we were on our way to the postseason, he was getting dialysis four times a day. But with the help of a friend, David Polachanin, he came to New York to see the Big East Tournament. He was ill, had a high fever, had to do his dialysis in the hotel, but he felt like he needed to be there. We got him a seat behind the bench, and I noticed on the last day of the Tournament that he wasn't there.

I called his parents, and they told me he was just too sick. He had to get back home.

We won the Big East Tournament, beat St. John's in the final, but we didn't cut down the nets at Madison Square Garden. We knew this team had bigger aspirations. We wanted to cut down the nets in St. Petersburg after winning our first championship. And we so much wanted Joe to be part of that. He had been on so much of the long road with us, the many tournament runs that had ended in disappointment in the 1990s. The NCAA sent us to the West Regional, first to Denver and then to Phoenix. I called Joe after the Selection Show and we talked for a good twenty minutes.

Joe was in Bristol Hospital, and I brought the team in to visit him. He wanted to talk about basketball, about the bracket. Players stationed themselves all around his bed, and someone complained about the travel, someone else complained about something else, the way players do. All of a sudden, Joe had heard enough.

"You guys think you have it tough?" he asked. Then he yanked off the blanket to drive home the point that he had lost his legs. His family, the players, me—there was total silence in that room. It was just an incredible moment. Joe did that because he didn't think about himself, he thought about *them*. He was thinking about *us*.

We hoped and prayed for the best for Joe McGinn as we headed to Denver. When we landed, I got the news. Joe McGinn had had a heart attack and died in his mother's arms. He had been fighting, his body had been fighting for so long. He just couldn't fight anymore. It was March 9, 1999. I gathered the players in Ricky Moore's room and gave them the news, and every one of them broke down.

I immediately got the watch I had been given for the Big East championship and sent it to his family. It was on his wrist as he was laid to rest. We couldn't go to the funeral, but when we took the long ride out to Colorado Springs for a practice at the Air Force Academy—I wanted us to practice at a high elevation before we played in Denver—I asked for a memorial service to be arranged. In the beautiful chapel they have out there, Captain Kent Johnson spoke as if he knew Joe, knew everything about him. Somehow he'd gotten the sense of who Joe McGinn was and what he had come to mean to all of us.

We beat Texas–San Antonio in the first round, which I had to miss because I had gotten ill out there, then beat New Mexico and shipped off to Phoenix, where we beat Iowa and Gonzaga to at long last break through to the Final Four.

Joe was watching, and smiling. We knew that. As his sister says, he was probably critiquing us every step of the way, grumbling that we'd had such a hard time in the Elite Eight game, winning by only 5 points.

When we got to St. Petersburg, the media became aware of Joe's story. "Just thinking of him gives me goose bumps," Jake Voskuhl told a reporter. Then Jake pointed to his legs to show them. "See, he is with this team right now."

We beat Ohio State, then won that nail-biter over Duke, 77–74, to win our first championship. As the buzzer sounded, I whispered to myself, "You knew it all the time, didn't you, Joe?"

Pat and I stay in touch with Joe's family. When his father was really struggling, Joe's mother called and asked me to talk to him. Hopefully, it helped. Since Joe's parents passed, his sister likes for me to tell her sons, both Division I football players, the stories about their uncle Joe, who they never knew.

So how do I begin to put my friendship with Joe McGinn into perspective after twenty-five years? When you can give something to somebody that costs you nothing, and yet it inspires you to realize how lucky *you* are? I guess it gave me joy that I could give him some.

The night I learned Joe died, I called his mother and said, "Joe will be in St. Petersburg. He'll have the best seat in the house." I told her I had "cheated her," because all those years she had talked about him getting inspiration from us, those were the things I got—that we all got—from Joe McGinn. He didn't have nearly enough days. But he made his days *count*.

Donny Marshall told me what he was going to do,
then went out and did it.

Credit: UConn

CHAPTER 12

Donny Marshall: The Tree Remembers

You build trust with few words, but all action.

> There is an old African proverb: *The ax forgets, the tree remembers.* That may sound like a negative thing, but with Coach, I think of that and it's kind of the inverse. The one who helps, he forgets. The one who has been helped, remembers. The tree remembers.
>
> —Donny Marshall

Every time he hails a taxi in New York, Boston, or whichever big city his life as a broadcaster leads him, Donny Marshall says he still thinks of me. More specifically, he thinks of the day we met.

Other coaches on the trail recruiting him apparently showed up in fancy rented cars, Cadillacs, maybe, and they'd bring several assistants with them. Donny and his mother lived in a small apartment in Federal Way, Washington, a Seattle suburb, and a full coaching staff would cram in there.

I arrived in a Yellow cab, alone. That's the way I traveled. It wasn't done to make a statement, but Donny is fifty now, and if that's what he remembers most, then I suppose it did. Maybe that's just part of my blue-collar, work-and-fight-for-everything-you-get background back in Braintree. I didn't put on airs, didn't move with an entourage.

The first thing I remember about Donny Marshall, he was a really good player, a unique player. He just didn't really have a defined position. He was one of the top soccer players in America, and he had been talking about playing professional soccer in Europe.

Howie Dickenman, my assistant, mentioned Donny to me. I asked if he could shoot, and Howie said, "No, not really."

"Is he a sky-above-the-rim rebounder?"

"He's okay," Howie replied. "He's not Scott Burrell."

"Well, can he handle the ball—run the floor exceptionally well?"

"No, not really."

"So what the hell does the kid do?" I asked.

"He competes like a *bastard*."

Okay, I was interested.

The first time I got in the house, I actually was amazed by how mature he was at age seventeen, which he was at the time. I mean, really mature. I think some of it had to do with being the father of the family to some degree, as I had to be at that age. His mom was working multiple jobs to keep a roof over their heads, a remarkable woman.

I wanted Donny to know he was special, that I wasn't just stopping by on a recruiting tour, so I didn't tell him I was coming from Los Angeles. I got off the plane, took a cab, and I was ready to spend as much time as I needed to tell him what a great place UConn is.

The idea of not bringing three assistants with me was to let players like Donny know that *I'm the guy* who's going to put you in a game, take you out of the game, start you, not start you, set things up for you or not set things up for you, so you better have a good trust and faith in me that I'm going to do it all for the right reasons. I've always felt the one thing I could do is get in front of somebody and be sincere, they can feel the emotion.

Donny was a guy who would talk to anybody. He was good-looking, charming; maybe the fact he was biracial had something to do with it. He knew how to get along with people, how to navigate the minefields that come with that. It may also have been part of the chip that was always on his shoulder. He had that "I'll show you" mentality.

I don't remember how long I was there, but the more I got to know him, the more I wanted him to be a basketball player and come to Connecticut. There was a toughness about him I kind of sensed, a kind of mental and physical toughness. I thought he could play in the Big East; I thought this kid could fit and help build the culture we were trying to build if I could just convince him to come 3,000 miles east from the Seattle suburbs to play in Storrs, Connecticut.

My message: *Donny, we need you. We need this kind of athlete to run our press, fast break*. Maybe seeing a guy get out of a cab without three assistants helped convey it. Apparently, it made a difference that day in Federal Way. Our relationship is a story about trust, and Donny and I grew to trust each other's words, because our actions were trustworthy.

I brought some videotapes of how we played at UConn, the NIT run in '88, the so-called "Dream Season," the way we got started. To show you how long ago this was, Donny's mom had to borrow a VCR so I could play them. I told them who we played against—Syracuse, Georgetown, St. John's. He'd only been playing basketball a short time, but he knew the brand names. I told him, you're going to play in big arenas.

"The only 'UConn' we knew about was in Alaska," Donny always jokes. That was a common thing you heard back then. Actually, the first NCAA Tournament game he'd ever watched was a pretty good one, the game we won on the Scottie Burrell pass to Tate George for the buzzer-beater against Clemson at the Meadowlands the previous March. We had what they now call "brand recognition."

It was about 9:30 in the morning, and we had a small breakfast. After a while, I asked Donny how he got to school every day, and he said he walked.

"So let's take a walk," I said.

It was about a ten-minute walk over the Pacific Highway, and he gave me a tour. Then we walked back, and I wanted to see the other places he hung out, the playground where he played basketball, the fields where he played soccer, the SeaTac Mall he'd frequent with his friends. We walked a couple of hours, at least.

When we got back to his home, his mother had lunch ready. I said, "Let's watch some tapes." As Donny can tell you, our motto then was "You can at UConn."

The great thing about Donny, he was very inquisitive. He wanted to know more. He said, "Where do you see me playing?" And I said, "On the court." I told him I played small forwards, big guards. Donny just kept the conversation going. You really had to be on top of your game with him.

I knew he was going to make a decision soon, and I kept pushing the basketball side of things. But it was as far away as you could get from Connecticut, 3,000 miles. I didn't make a whole lot of promises about basketball, about minutes, about a professional future. I promised something more; I promised that when he came back to those places, the playground, the mall, that we had walked to, the kids would still be there doing the same things, but Donny would be in a different place.

I didn't say anything about the NBA. I didn't think in those terms; I wanted to make Donny and his mother promises I could keep.

His mother asked why I wanted to see all the places Donny hung out, and I told her, "Because my job is not just to make him a better basketball player. When I return him to you, he's going to be a *man.* And not just any man, he's going to be a great man. All those places we walked to, where he hung out, he was a child. When he comes back, I'm going to make sure I help him become the best man he can be."

She was a single mother, like my mom had become. I had a feel for what she would want for Donny, and it resonated with her. We had the connection, and she knew I was going to be there for her son.

So Donny came to UConn. He was 6-foot-7, over 200 pounds, when he got to campus in the summer of 1991. We put ourselves on the national stage with our terrific season in 1990, what some came to call the Dream Season, and we followed that with another NCAA trip in '91, but our designs were bigger. Donny arrived with a huge incoming class. Donny, Donyell Marshall, Kevin Ollie, Brian Fair, Nate Willingham, Richie Ashmeade, Rudy Johnson, my son Jeff—eight new guys added to what we had, Scottie Burrell, Chris Smith, still UConn's scoring leader, Rod Sellers, Dan Cyrulik. A culture isn't about one team or one season; it has to be maintained. Ours was coming together, and starting to move from season to season, core group to core group.

When everybody sat down, after a long practice in a sweltering gym, our old field house, the young players were wearing gray T-shirts with UCONN stamped on them; players would joke they looked like prison attire. When they worked hard enough, they earned the high-end—well, higher-end—Starter-brand practice apparel. I gave them the speech I always give the newcomers. Donny remembers it well; they all do. "There was a man who came to your home and sold you on this place. Told you some great things. Maybe promised you a couple of things. That man? *You will never see him again.*"

As Donny says, I didn't lie then; I never lied again.

The freshman year was rough for a soccer player on the basketball court. Donny had some deficiencies, couldn't do much going to his left, but he was the fighter I recognized back in Federal Way. The hardest part was keeping him off the soccer field, convincing him he was a basketball player now; he had to devote his energies to that. It's not like we were splitting the scholarship.

We went 20–10, back to the NCAA Tournament, where we lost to Ohio State in the second round. Donny played only about 9 minutes a game, and he was doing all this talking, and I was thinking, "How 'bout being a freaking player first?" At the end of the season, he sat down in my office and I told him, "Maybe you should go back home and play in the Pac-12. Your game might be more suited to that." Oh, he had the size and the spirit to play in the rugged Big East, as rugged then as it ever was, but he had to be challenged.

You can't treat every player the same. Any coach who says that is kidding you, or themselves. You can *care* about all of them the same, but you have to find out what they will respond to, and what they won't. If Donny had to play angry, so be it. I've been known to make people angry on occasion.

So Donny sat down for his postseason meeting and I suggested he move on. We had a lot of great players in front of him and I was going to recruit more, I told him. I offered to call other coaches to find a place where he could play on the West Coast.

He left, went to call home and talk it over with his mom. Would he take me up on it? Would he give up basketball and go play soccer after all? His mom told him he'd made a commitment and he needed to go prove the coach wrong.

Donny came back to my office and said he was going to stay—that he loved UConn, loved his teammates. He told me three things: He was going to be captain of this team someday; he was going to be one of the most memorable players I'd ever coach at UConn; and he was going to play in the NBA. I smiled a little and said, "Okay, show me how you're going to do that."

That's exactly what Donny Marshall did. He accepted the challenge. His sophomore year, he was a different guy, different player.

He stayed, learned how to be a basketball player, not just an athlete, and he went on to do all he'd promised to do, including graduating on time, in 1995.

Donny told me he was going to run a mile in under five minutes when we had our annual "Husky Run." He did that. Said what he was going to do, and did it. It wasn't always easy. I had to get him to react physically, which was not the natural tendency for him. His tendency was to say something back. He never did, but he'd say it under his breath.

You know, Donny had diarrhea of the mouth at times, kept running his mouth when he shouldn't have. He had to look at my face to figure out I wasn't just pushing this time, I really meant it. We got to that point a few times, but one thing I'd never say about Donny is that he's not smart. He'd tell you today, "I needed that."

His mom knew. She loved Donny to a fault, as all mothers should, but she seemed to know what he needed, and she had told me, "When he gets to campus, he's yours." As a coach, you don't forget when a mother trusts you with her son.

There came a time, we were playing Villanova, and I was hollering something out to Donny, maybe not using the gentlest of language, and Kerry Kittles sidled up to him and said, "When Calhoun yells at you, it's bad for us."

Donny was a significant player as a sophomore, a starter as a junior and senior. We were 57–10 those two seasons, 28–5, 29–5. Back to the Elite Eight in 1995. What was once considered a Dream Season was becoming the standard UConn season. Culture. Donny and his class were a big part of that.

Donny was a guy you cared about by evolution; the more you were with him, the more you saw him not only grow, but understand things from your perspective—he's got some similarities with you. When he's upset, he lets you know. You know what I say? When I've got shit in my mouth, I say "shit." I started to appreciate him over a period of time. I was watching Donny grow as a man and, as part of this deal, helping *me* grow. Our relationship evolved over those years. Donny says we were just too much alike not to connect. He wasn't the last player to say that. Maybe there were times when I might cringe to hear it, but—he was never perfect, but the good thing was, he played for a coach who wasn't perfect, either.

By his junior year, he knew that he could trust his worth ethic. Maybe I couldn't trust his mouth. His senior year, he wore it as a badge of honor. He says that I was protecting him on the sidelines and he was protecting himself on the court. It wasn't in his job description to bark at officials, but he did it anyway.

Donny Marshall had promised his mother he would stay the course at UConn and graduate. When that day came, his graduation ceremony as a communications major was at a different time than the other players who were graduating, so he was the team's only representative at that particular ceremony, where his mother and older brother, home from his military service, were beaming in the crowd. To this day, he counts it as one of his greatest memories, walking across that stage in a cap and gown and hearing that ovation.

Captain? Check. Memorable career at UConn? Check. Next—he had to work for it, but he made it three for three—he played in the NBA. Drafted in the second round in 1995, he stayed until 2003, then stayed in the game as a broadcaster. He has worked more than 1,300 college and pro games, with the Celtics, the Nets, the Olympics. Occasionally, he does some UConn games, and, speaking his mind as always, he'll ruffle some feathers among Huskies fans.

There was one promise I didn't quite keep to Donny's mom. I had promised to send him back to Federal Way as a man, and I think he grew into manhood quicker than most. But he didn't go back to Federal Way. I had also told him that once he got to Connecticut, became part of our culture, he might not want to live anywhere else.

He may have thought I was nuts, but he still lives in Connecticut today. And he became a man who wanted to see more of the world.

I realize that the gift of coaching is communicating. One day, years after he played for me, he said, "Love you, Coach." It wasn't a big deal at the time, but the more I thought about it, the more I realized that when I told him he should leave UConn—I wasn't actually throwing him out of school, but I told him, "If you want to be a better player, you have to learn to keep your mouth shut." Then I watched him evolve. I'm really proud of Donny for a lot of different things; knowing about his life, growing up without a father, we shared a lot in our lives without ever talking about that.

He was handsome, he was articulate, and he knew that these things were weapons, because he could really do things with that personality, and it's kind of funny he makes a living doing it now on TV. Once I kind of figured him out, though, it was not a surprise. It's been pretty special to watch this kid—who a lot of people liked as a player, charming as heck, the whole package—evolve into a man, a wonderful husband and father with three daughters and a son.

Whatever Ray Allen does, he expects to do it flawlessly.

Credit: UConn

CHAPTER 13

Ray Allen: An Acquired Taste

Good, better, best. Never let it rest until
your "good" becomes your best.

With Coach Calhoun, you can't hold back. You've got to give everything; you've got to commit to the whole ball of wax. He always knew when we weren't giving anything. You just couldn't perform under him, be under his umbrella, if you didn't give everything. But once you let it go and you give everything? Then who you're supposed to be comes out....Competing, really competing, being a competitor and beating the guy next to me, is something he taught all of us. Every single day, you've got to want to win as badly as you want to breathe.

—Ray Allen

Players have said all kinds of things about me, most of them kind, but my favorite quote is probably something Ray Allen said to me once at the Hall of Fame in Springfield. "Coach, you're the best coach I've ever had...*but you're an acquired taste*." I guess that can be taken a few ways, but I choose to believe it means I kind of grow on people.

It didn't take long for Ray Allen to grow on me. You know, he retired as the greatest 3-point shooter in the history of the game, his ticket to the Hall of Fame, but I saw him play as a teenager in the program at Riverside Church in New York City, where he scored 62 points—without a 3-pointer. He didn't have that in his arsenal then. I just couldn't believe what a magnificent athlete he was.

Walter Ray Allen was such a phenomenal athlete, it may be hard to think of him as "self-made." His mother, Flo, and his father, Walter Ray Sr., were both great athletes. I once saw his father playing a one-on-one game against one of our staffers, and at age forty-eight, his dad was quick as a cat.

Yet I saw Ray as self-made. He was driven, and he made himself into a great shooter—the greatest—enhancing his natural gifts. Around UConn, they remember Ray's game-winning shot against Georgetown in the Big East Tournament. We'll get to that. Worldwide, he's remembered for the 3-pointer he made for Miami, in Game 6 of the NBA Finals in 2013, forcing a Game 7, which the Heat won. You look at that shot, and it tells you all you need to know about Ray Allen. Everything was very calculated: He knew exactly where he was, where his feet were; he knew the time remaining, and the situation. I don't know if he dreamed about doing something like that, but it wouldn't surprise me, because that's how he saw himself.

Ray grew up in a military family, born on an air force base in California, moving numerous times. He would often get a laugh when people wondered aloud why, when he came to UConn from Dalzell, South Carolina, he didn't have a Southern accent. He liked structure, he liked discipline, he liked accountability.

A lot of big schools wanted him. He often tells the story of visiting Kentucky, having a meal with some other recruits and coaches, and Rick Pitino was at another table. He noted that at UConn, I would have been bringing them their Cokes. (He's right about that; I don't know how other coaches did it, but as others have described, I always tried to be myself, down-to-earth, whether it was arriving by taxi without an entourage or, yes, getting up to bring a kid his soda.)

When Ray visited Connecticut, we made sure someone was with him every minute, making sure he knew how badly we wanted him. He says this was different from his visits to other campuses. He also liked the chemistry and culture on our team; he found the players had a "healthy fear" of the consequences of not being in shape, not doing what they were supposed to be doing.

"In college sports, the head coach of a program is about to be your new dad," Ray says. "When it came to Coach, he was a very staunch disciplinarian; he wanted things done a certain way. And I really took to it, because that's how I grew up. Accountability. You would see one or two guys transfer out every year because they didn't want to be accountable."

He was the most inquisitive player I ever coached. He asked about everything, wanted to know how anything and everything worked. After Howie Dickenman had made the first contact, where Ray had made a positive impression, I went to visit him for the first time. I was wearing a basketball-themed necktie that Jim Valvano had designed, ties that were sold to raise funds for the Jimmy V. Foundation and all the great work it does for cancer research. Ray kept asking about it; he was fascinated with the tie. This wasn't, and I'm sure still isn't, the usual experience of a first meeting with a seventeen-year-old.

He would sometimes ask: "Coach, do you think your tie goes with that suit?" He wasn't being critical; he simply thought about such things. And he was the same way with his teammates. When Doron Sheffer came from Israel to join us, Ray wanted to get to know him, and everything about him. He began studying Jewish history, the Holocaust. He wanted to know about all of it. After his playing days, in 2017, Ray made a trip to Auschwitz and wrote a moving piece about his experiences for *The Players' Tribune*. One of the most insightful people I've ever known, always on a quest to learn.

When he made his movie with Denzel Washington in 1998, *He Got Game*, Ray made sure to take diction classes. He spoke just fine, but he was never going to be unprepared for anything he was doing. That was Ray.

The pastoral setting of Storrs—even more so in the early 1990s than you would find it today—also agreed with Ray. He liked the lack of distractions, didn't need a city or a beach nearby, wanted to be surrounded by teammates. He wanted to concentrate on basketball, and UConn was the place to do it. It's funny, Stephon Castle, who played one season for the Huskies, winning a championship in 2023 and then going to the Spurs with the fourth pick in the NBA Draft, said many of the same things. For a certain type of player, saying "There's not much to do in Storrs" was not a negative, but a positive.

Ray chose us over Kentucky, and he arrived at Storrs in 1993. While some kids didn't know what "agenda" meant, Ray Allen had one. When he said "I want to be great," he wasn't shitting you. He was committed to that. He was developing a way to get where he needed to be, and he got there.

Maybe Ray Allen and I just crossed paths at a perfect time. I was forty-nine when he got to UConn; I had been a Coach of the Year; I had built the UConn program from the bottom of the Big East to the top, won the NIT, reached the Elite Eight during the Dream Season, but we hadn't gotten to a Final Four, so, like Ray, I was driven to achieve more. Playing for me, you weren't going to get Mr. Sunshine all the time. You're not going to get the guy that starts all the jokes. You're going to know what you have to do, you're going to do it to the best of your ability, and if that's not good enough, then turn the lights on at eleven p.m.; I'll be back in the gym.

In his first game with us, Ray remembers he was sitting on the bench. He noticed a lot of the older players had towels in their hands. He didn't know why, until a player missed a layup and I went crazy, marching down the bench hollering, "He's a stiff! He's a stiff!" In the heat of the moment, I could be like that, and the players with the towels, Rudy Johnson, Brian Fair, were ready; they had something to bite down on to keep from laughing. Ray, unaccustomed to my in-game demeanor, burst out laughing, and I glowered at him. I guess that's what he meant by my being an "acquired taste."

Ray says I was "the most underrated coach in America" at that time. He could see how badly I wanted UConn to be mentioned among the great, storied programs (the term "blue bloods" wasn't fashionable yet), and he wanted to help us get there.

I told him my Oscar Robertson story. Oscar would take a basketball, dribble it all the way to school, dribble it all the way home. So Ray's freshman year, he had a basketball all the time, on the bus, to his dorm and back. I might get upset with Ray now and again, but I could never question his work ethic. As a freshman, Ray came off the bench and averaged 12.6 points per game, and only made one 3-pointer in his thirty-four games. That skill was still coming.

He believes I held him to a "different standard," and in some ways, maybe I did. You see, Ray had the greatness, and if I saw something less than that, if I saw him slack off on defense, for instance, or let one part of his game go, I would stress to him that I wasn't going to let him get away with that—where another coach might—because I believed he was simply too good to play that way, to do "just enough." He responded to that approach.

I stressed to him that he had a chance to not only be great, but to be one of the greatest *ever*, if he would commit to the process. He was smart enough to recognize that. He wanted to be extraordinary in everything he did, and I just reminded him of that every time I needed to.

Sometimes people considered him standoffish. He just didn't suffer fools gladly, still doesn't, and he was very purposeful about everything he did. Never had a great desire to be one of the boys. He's bright. He does great things. He's in the Hall of Fame. Very few like him in my fifty years of coaching. "Ray," I'd tell him, "we just practiced two hours. You've been shooting for an hour, your hands are going to start bleeding pretty soon." His quest for greatness was off the charts. He was going to find a way to be great.

A lot of kids would say, "Just let me shoot the ball," but that wasn't going to be Ray Allen's way. He wanted to know everything about the mechanics of shooting, getting every move and twitch right, as our coach Glen Miller, who knows the craft so well, worked with him. The result was a shot that started at the tips of his toes, up through his long lean body to his fingertips, and the perfect release of the ball.

As a sophomore, Ray started and averaged 21.1 points per game. By now he was getting off six 3-point shots per game and making just about half of them. We went 28–5; Ray, Doron, Kevin Ollie, Donny Marshall, Travis Knight, and we lost to UCLA in Oakland in the Elite Eight. Ray scored 36 points in that game.

We were very close. His first two years, he was in my office every day to chat about something. His third year, he had some things going on in his life, the NBA was now an inevitability, and he was focused on getting as much as he could out of his time in college. He was on track and he never got off track. He averaged 23.4 points per game, shot 47 percent on 3s, and we reached the Sweet 16.

But the climactic moment of that season, and the signature of Ray's UConn career, came in New York in the Big East Tournament, March 9, 1996.

Ray played well in the first half, but missed 14 shots in a row in the second half. Ricky Moore and Kirk King had great second halves to keep us close. We were down a point during a timeout with about 30 seconds to go. Ray looked dejected. But I drew up a play for him, for Ricky to get him the ball. "I was like, 'Oh, snap, he expects me to win this game for him," Ray remembers. "Coach didn't even hesitate."

Well, he *was* the Big East player of the year; I wouldn't have cared if he missed 80 in a row. As you've learned by now, when I believed in someone, I believed, and I let them know it when they most needed to know it. Ricky got him the ball, and Ray looked over at his friend, Rudy Johnson, who looked away. In midair, Ray turned toward the basket and shot his contested shot. It went in with 13.6 seconds left. When Georgetown didn't score, Ray came running down the court full speed, ran past me, and knocked over our manager, Karen Ewald. That was one time when Ray Allen, elegant, handsome, cool, just let all his emotions hang out.

We kept knocking on the door to the Final Four, but we didn't get there or win a championship while Ray Allen was at UConn. Still, he did as much as anyone to lay the foundation for the six that came, beginning in 1999. I'm always thrilled to see my guys gathering to watch the current team, especially at the Final Fours. It's very special, and it's important to me that they feel a part of it. Guys like Ray, they began building the culture of championships, the culture of "how we do things."

Ray entered the pros after his junior year and was the fifth pick in the 1996 NBA Draft, ending up with Milwaukee, where he started his eighteen-year career, 1,300 games. Always in superb shape, always prepared, always adapting as the game changed, his teams and his roles changed, and his game changed, the 3-pointer becoming a bigger part of it as he got to the Celtics in 2007, as it became a bigger and bigger part of the way the game was played in the NBA. He won championships with Boston, and then in Miami, where he played with LeBron James.

Always proud of his work ethic, Ray and Kobe Bryant actually used to feud about who worked harder. It's not that Ray thought he was better than anybody else; he knew he was *going* to be better than anybody else. He's a guy that put himself in the Hall of Fame. He set himself apart. He was going to beat you, he was going to outwork you. And he did. He never thought he was good enough, never stopped to pat himself on the back. He didn't rest until his very best was an everyday occurrence. His good became his best.

Having gone to UConn and playing and working within our structure prepared Ray well for the NBA. Like all my guys, he kept in touch and we would catch up. Always incredibly loyal to me, he'd do anything I asked him. Ray didn't need a whole lot of basketball advice from me at that point. He was a competitor; I didn't necessarily instill that in him, I just helped bring it out.

When Ray retired as a player, he was thirty-eight and could still outplay kids fifteen to twenty years younger. He made 2,973 3-pointers in the league, 40 percent of the 3s he took across all those years. Perhaps others have since broken—or will eventually break—some of his records, but to me, he's the greatest shooter there has ever been. (I'm a bit biased, of course, because I know what went into it.) Of all the players I've coached, all the players who have played the game, he's the greatest shooter. Think about that.

Always true to who he is, Ray doesn't show any weaknesses. Sometimes, in some places, that could be misunderstood; it was just that his drive showed. His incredible drive showed in everything he did his whole life, and he expects those around him to do the same.

A couple of years ago, Ray kept his promise to his mom, and was inspired by his daughter to earn his degree at UConn. What a proud moment that was, just as it was for Khalid and many others who have done it. Ray deserved that degree for the way he has led his life.

He coached his son's high school team in Florida. Just like at UConn, he would make sure his players boxed out and shot free throws before and after practice, challenges, competitions. I used to want my players to be lined up, clapping, showing energy as practice was about to begin. I wanted to see that they wanted to be there. Ray's kids did the same; he wanted them *ready* for practice, just as he always was on my teams.

But always, Ray judges himself harder than he judges other people. Some people didn't see that, but I did. He has always chased something he may never find: perfection. I guess, in this way, you could say that Ray Allen is an acquired taste, too. And I've always been grateful we acquired each other.

Ben Gordon is in a fight, and he will have me by his side every step of the way.

Credit: UConn

CHAPTER 14

Ben Gordon: UConn's Silent Assassin

There's a reason the front window of a car is bigger than the rear.

> You see how compassionate Coach has become. He really created a family environment at UConn, and he is still very much in touch with his players. I remember a lot of conversations with Coach over the years; sometimes I wasn't doing so well, other times I'd be doing great, and either way he was there when I just wanted to talk to somebody. He's always someone I can rely on.
>
> —Ben Gordon

I was at Seton Hall's gym in New Jersey on a Sunday morning for an AAU game, sitting next to Mike Krzyzewski. We were watching this one player, and Mike looked at me and said, "Gee, this kid is a nice player, what a great body, but I'm not sure what he is."

As coaches, we all do that, say things like that. We'll look at a kid's build, his skills, and we see the talent, but we can't picture him playing a specific position. I might say, "He's not a point guard," and one of my coaches advocating for a player would say, "Yeah, but he's a *player*." All of us have our stereotypes, prototypes, for certain positions.

The player Mike and I were talking about was Ben Gordon, about 6-foot-3, skinny, explosive. A scorer, a shooter, phenomenal athlete. But what was he? Ben didn't seem to fit perfectly into one position or another, but he had this unique ability to stand still, take the elevator up to the second floor, and get his jump shot. He'd catch the ball and just go above other people and shoot.

So we were talking. What position would he eventually fill? And I was thinking, *Someplace on the court*. He didn't have the appearance of a great player, maybe, but, wow, he was a great player. To me, the biggest question about a basketball player is "Can he get his own?" Ben could get his own. And when he got his own, he didn't miss. Could he shoot! He was introverted, a silent assassin, I called him.

My assistants Karl Hobbs and Dave Leitao and I made numerous trips to Mount Vernon, New York, just over the border from Connecticut, to see him. I wanted to make sure Ben saw how badly we wanted him—that if other schools might be unsure about where he'd play, we knew he'd play for us. He knew the Big East, wanted to stay close to home, play in The Garden. He came to Storrs to visit and I rolled out the heavy artillery: I took him across campus to the famous Dairy Bar for ice cream, and we talked for real as the cows were grazing nearby.

"I saw another side of the coach," Ben remembers now. "I got to know him a little bit. He was straightforward with me. He let me know they would be playing a pro type system and it would help me going forward. And pretty much everything he said to expect when I came to UConn was spot-on."

So Ben came to UConn and roomed with Emeka Okafor, and I'm sure it was an unusual room in many ways. Both were really, really smart and they formed a really deep relationship. Mek was obsessed with finding out why something worked and how it worked. With Ben, you kind of gave him what it was, told him "This is how you do it," and you didn't have to say another word.

Ben's mom worked for General Electric, and he was born in London, England, before moving with his family to Mount Vernon, New York, where he led his high school team to championships and became a top-forty recruit. He had personality, but he was a quiet kid, into himself. He did well with things where he could self-motivate—shooting the ball, for example; when he made his mind up about something, he became obsessed with it. He could be funny, but I learned very quickly that if you gave him a challenge, consider him *challenged.* Ben was going to go after it. As a freshman, he averaged 12.6 points for us. We figured out how to use him.

Early in his sophomore year, we were playing Vanderbilt, and we were down 6 points, with 6 minutes to go, down there in Nashville. I called a time-out. Ben hadn't scored, an 18-point-a-game scorer at the time, and I just lit into him. If we had 3 minutes, I spent 2 minutes and 59 seconds reminding him he hadn't scored. He goes out to get 8 of the last 9 points, and we won 76–70. Sometimes, you just had to let him know how good he was.

"Coach would always put it in my head, 'Hey, Ben, we need you to score, we need you to shoot, we need you to be more aggressive,' " Ben says. "He just had a way of helping me see the game through his lens."

And he never overreacted to anything like that. He just got better and better and better. His junior year, he averaged 20 points per game, and it was assumed by everyone, everywhere, that he was going to be a high pick in the NBA Draft. Ben got into a little slump during the season, and with that good a team, a team good enough to win it all, I took notice of any sign of a slip.

Ben reminded me of this story: I called him into my office and sat him down, we looked at some mock drafts, and I asked him, "Hey, how are your grades?" He looked a little confused, like, "Why is he asking me about academics now?" He said fine. So I asked a few more questions about what courses he was taking and how they were going. Finally, he asked what I was driving at.

"Well, you might want to focus on that," I told him, "because the way you're playing, you might have to return next year." I started telling him about guys playing overseas, things I knew he didn't want to hear. Sounds like me. He says that lit a little fire under him. He and Emeka led us to our second championship, decisively won. Ben was most outstanding player of the Big East Tournament and the Phoenix Regional, and led the NCAA Tournament in scoring. In the Draft, Charlotte took Emeka at No. 2, and the Bulls took Ben at No. 3.

The NBA game was more open, more spacing, and I knew Ben was well prepared for it. He had the toughness, the edge. He was the NBA's sixth man of the year as a rookie, and went on to have a productive eleven seasons in the League. We would stay in touch, off and on, talk about life, the good times, the bad times. He learned he could kid me around a little, could ask me for advice on being a father, about finances. Occasionally, we'd talk about basketball.

"Every time you pick up the phone with him, even if it's been a while, it's like you never miss a beat," Ben says. "It's good to have people in your life who are reliable, who never change. The vibe's always the same."

As his career wound down, Ben's life was going to change, as it does for any player. He had that orderly life of practices and games; he didn't have a lot of free time. He was always in control of things, handled his money wisely, so careful about anything he put in his body; he wouldn't even take a piece of gum without knowing what was in it. He was a purebred athlete, meticulous about being great.

After his career ended, he had more time and didn't really know what was next. I started to get word from some of his teammates that he was having some problems, and one player sent me a photo that concerned me. He looked very gaunt, not like the guy I knew. I called him and asked if he was okay, and he said, "Yeah, just having some fun, Coach." He would always assure me that everything was fine.

In February 2020, Ben published an essay in *The Players' Tribune*, accompanied by a similar photo, which was captioned "Where is my mind?" It began "There was a point in time when I thought about killing myself every single day for about six weeks..." Ben went on to detail his struggles with mental health and his fight to regain control of his life.

I was shocked, heartbroken for him, but I couldn't have been prouder of him for the courage he showed, the willingness not only to confront it, but to tell his story so that it might help others going through similar things. I wanted him to know I was in his corner, as ever. I was in touch with his mom, who'd come up to see me at Saint Joseph's.

"When you're done playing, it's an adjustment," Ben says. "You've done something for so long, and now you're not really sure what you want to do next or what your options are. It can drive you nuts. I've had some ups and downs since I finished my career, some misunderstandings, when I've been in the wrong place at the wrong time. But Coach has always been supportive, just there for me when I didn't have so many people to talk to. He was always in my corner. He always came to me with understanding."

There were stories in the papers, videos out there on the internet of various episodes, and again, this wasn't the Ben Gordon I knew. I didn't recognize him. And for about five months, I couldn't get through to him. I'd always called him if I went a week or two without hearing from him, and we'd talk about everything going on in his life. Now I kept trying to reach him without success. I was getting more and more worried about him. Pat, in her wisdom, kept telling me, "When he's ready, when he really needs you, he'll call." He was one of my guys. I'd call certain people who knew where he was to try to get some news.

Finally, he called. He reached out and said he wanted to make sure I had his new phone number. He was getting help; he was winning his fight. UConn was planning to honor the 2004 championship team, celebrating the twentieth anniversary on January 28, 2024, and I knew Ben had to be there. He hadn't been around UConn for a long time. There was a spot in the Huskies of Honor waiting for him, but during his pro playing days he was unable to get there. The spot was still waiting. This could be a first step in getting him back in the UConn family. Now, his teammates would be waiting, too.

"We need you," I told him over and over. "I need you there. You're like a son to me."

There was a calmness about him now. He agreed to come, and told me he had a plane ticket. I'd ask what time he was getting in and he wouldn't know. I knew what that meant—that he didn't really have a ticket—but I kept after him. A few days before the event, he gave me an ETA. He was coming.

Ben arrived in Hartford on Saturday night. When I called he was at the steakhouse in Hartford with all the guys. He was laughing, and I heard more laughter in the background. They'd been to practice that day. Ben was home. He was with family. Every one of those guys was asking for his new number. They were group-texting with the guys who couldn't make it to town.

The next morning, I joined the group for breakfast before we all headed to the XL Center for the UConn game and the ceremony. Ben was smiling, talking, and I felt so good. We both knew he couldn't have missed this.

Professional basketball is a business, sometimes cold, but your college team is different, the relationships are different. Ben joined his former teammates, his brothers Emeka Okafor, Taliek Brown, Rashad Anderson, and Shamon Tooles, and coaches George Blaney and Andre LaFleur, in an auxiliary locker room in the basement of the arena. He was surrounded by reporters, some of whom had covered him when he played for UConn. He was calm and confident, eloquently and gracefully handling the questions thrown at him.

"I'm in a good place," he said, and everyone was relieved, especially me. He looked as if he could have suited up and dropped 20 points on Xavier that day.

When they introduced him I got goosebumps during the ovation he received from the UConn fans. I wanted him to feel the love. This wasn't a one-and-done kid; Ben spent three years at UConn. If he was looking for love, he found it. People loved him in Connecticut. He had a warm smile as he walked out holding our national championship trophy for a photo. After the game, he was one of the alums who visited the current team in the locker room. "And he had some awesome things to say," Dan Hurley said.

We've been in touch more regularly in the months since. My hope is for Ben to get himself back out there. I'm hoping he finishes his degree at UConn, as a number of my former players have been doing. He doesn't have much more to do, and he has so much to offer.

"Just doing stuff and enjoying life, that's what he's trying to get me to do," Ben says. "Trying to enjoy this beautiful life that we have the privilege to live."

Ben thinks about things very deeply. What's next? Maybe he's not ready for what's next, and that's cool, too. He's looking for that. There's nothing Ben Gordon can't do, if he sets his mind and heart on it.

It's okay to look back. Ben Gordon had a wonderful basketball career, and he made great friends who care about him. But there's a reason the front window on a car is bigger than the rear; it faces what's coming up in the future, all that life has in store for us. I was thrilled when Ben and UConn got together on a date, February 6, 2025, for him to return to Gampel Pavilion and take his rightful place in the Huskies of Honor. I don't have the depth of knowledge or insight to fully understand what Ben is going through, but I know he's in a fight, and I know he's going to win it. The same way he became a great player, he's going to conquer this.

And he knows I'm going to be right there beside him.

Mark Daigneault, NBA Coach of the Year in 2024.

Credit: Oklahoma City Thunder

AFTERWORD

"He Puts Wind in Your Sails"

By Mark Daigneault

Mark Daigneault, now thirty-nine, was a student manager under Jim Calhoun at UConn from 2003 to 2007. He's now the head coach of the NBA's Oklahoma City Thunder. In his fourth season, 2023–24, he led his team to a 57–25 record, the best in the Western Conference, and to the conference semifinals. He was named NBA Coach of the Year.

It's about 140 miles from Storrs to New York City, somewhere around a three-hour drive on winding highways and through small Northeast towns, eventually breaking open to the endless skyline of Manhattan. It's a trip very familiar to the Huskies, a yearly March trek to Madison Square Garden for the Big East Tournament.

Prior to the 2005 tournament, about thirty minutes or so before we were set to board our bus and make the journey south, Coach Calhoun pulled me aside and had one of the longest conversations he'd ever had with me, up to that point: "I need you to drive my car to the hotel," he said, putting the keys to a white Ford Expedition in my hand. "Follow the bus."

Just for good measure, he added one more very clear instruction: "And don't screw it up."

This wasn't as uncomplicated as it sounds. For a twenty-year-old sophomore at UConn, from Leominster, Massachusetts, the thought of driving into Manhattan was daunting enough, but here I'd be driving a very large, very expensive car that was not mine, that just so happened to belong to one of the greatest college basketball coaches of all time. He wanted it in New York for some reason, and it was my job to get it there. While also, if you forgot, not screwing it up.

With my buddy Ben Wood riding shotgun, I got behind the wheel and pulled in behind the bus, sitting across from Gampel Pavilion, on a street now known as Jim Calhoun Way. There were already enough variables to make this a stressful job for a student manager, but there's an important twist: We had this bus driver named Walter, and to put it simply, he drove like a maniac. He was an elite bus driver, but he drove a 50-foot-long bus like it was a Toyota Corolla—fast, and aggressively. Speed limits were just numbers on metal signs to Walter; yellow lights were invitations to hit the gas.

At the XL Center in Hartford, the underground garage has a sharp dogleg, and has induced plenty of insurance claims to prove it. Walter, though, would cut those turns like he was showing off in an empty parking lot, never slowing down or ever reversing, but always coming out the other side clean and without a scratch. He was part chauffeur, part maniac, full bus-driving badass.

Walter had the reigning national champs on board, and he was going to get from northeast Connecticut to Manhattan without wasting a second. Again, this is 2005, before Google maps. I had no idea where I was going, so Ben and I had to tail Walter to New York City, with Coach's very clear instructions rattling in my head the entire time. In the year and a half I'd been with the UConn team, Coach hadn't said much to me, but now here I was driving his car, my hands white-knuckled at 10 and 2, my first big chance to do something of value for him.

After going west on US-44 to Hartford, then I-84 to I-91 South, then Hutchinson River Parkway into New York, then NY-9A to Henry Hudson Parkway, with about a thousand turns in between, we made it into the city. We were trying to keep up with Walter through the maze of Manhattan—honking horns, tight streets, cars everywhere merging and parking—to our hotel near Madison Square Garden, but he'd somehow get blocks in front of us. It felt hopeless. He'd run every light he could, somehow wiggling that bus through every street, with Ben and I squinting ahead in desperate search of it. "Is that the bus? Is that it? There it is!"

We got to our hotel, pulled into the garage, and, for the first time in three hours, I exhaled. Ben, who is now an assistant coach at Central Connecticut, was simply a friendly acquaintance when he sat down in the front seat, but by the time I triumphantly handed Coach his keys back in the lobby, we had become best friends. We still are to this day.

That was the "Coach Calhoun Experience" in a nutshell: You were simultaneously empowered and scared to death. When he's testing out his trust, he puts pressure on you. He puts you in the game, and now it's on you to make it happen. It's an elixir of emotions that gets you to a place where you're optimally able to perform, because you have a high level of urgency, and a high level of his confidence. I saw him do that again and again, and at the time, I didn't know what I was watching. But those memories are vivid to me, and I'm still learning lessons from my time at UConn, even though I'm no longer there.

I played basketball at Leominster High, and when I graduated, I wanted to coach. My high school coach, Steve Dubzinski, knew George Blaney, the associate head coach at UConn, and that's how I got my foot in the door as a student manager in 2003.

I started working with the program, mainly with Coach Blaney for the first year or so. He would give me projects because he knew I wanted to coach. I would help him with compiling his game notes, organizing our summer camps, and completing other logistical tasks. Coach Calhoun was aware of me, but the first year or so, he didn't talk to me very much. Eventually, he learned my name, which was sort of an initiation process he would do with the managers. Many of us would be involved with the program, so he distributed his trust judiciously. He needed time to feel you out before he'd let you all the way in.

Gradually, I started to get more involved with the staff, and with him. I was in the gym with the players a lot—in the summer, in the preseason, after hours during the season—working with them, rebounding for them, sweating with them. I had my sleeves rolled up with the guys, but I was also a coaching apprentice, and that caught his eye. He started sending subtle signals to the players and the other staff members: "This is a person I trust. This is a person you should be taking seriously."

Of course, you're still going to be getting his coffee, with the perfect amount of cream. But he had a way of empowering you that made you feel seen—that made you feel important to the program. He did it at strategic times and in an authentic way. And that put wind in your sails.

Soon, he began telling me his stories—the players he admired, the historic games he'd coached, the funny anecdotes—and it gave me a strong sense of belonging. It was him saying, "You're part of the tribe." I was working basically full-time. When I wasn't in class, I was there, and he knew that I was after something. Sometimes, there was a pat on the back. Sometimes, it was his foot up my ass.

In my sophomore year, I was working with Coach Blaney on our scouting reports, and we had a game at Gampel against Pittsburgh. They had Chevon Troutman, Carl Krauser, Aaron Gray, and we lost, uncharacteristically. They were better that day, but you just don't lose at Gampel if you're a UConn basketball team.

Now Coach Calhoun is not exactly a sunshine-and-rainbows kind of person as it is, so after a game like that, the last person you wanted to make eye contact with was him. I was standing off the court, quietly and innocently, and he popped me. I forgot precisely what he said, but it included his favorite word. I was in his line of fire. It was that two-sided coin again: urgency and empowerment.

You're a college undergrad and you feel like, "All right, I'm getting hit, too. I'm part of the team," and, "I hope this doesn't mean I'm fired." In this very bizarre way, you feel that wind in your sails—and like a lion is chasing you.

As my senior year was winding down, the 2007 season, I learned of an opening on the coaching staff at Holy Cross. Here I was, twenty-two years old, and I had a chance at the job, partly because Coach Blaney had coached there previously, but also because Coach Calhoun knew Coach Ralph Willard, a former rival at Pitt and the current coach at Holy Cross. I'll never forget how hard he worked to help me get that job. I had just graduated. There were players on the Holy Cross team who were older than I. But I was offered the job, and I always thought it had to do with how hard Coach Calhoun was willing to push for me. He was working the phone, multiple times, and following up with Coach Willard. It was almost like that was my salary for working for the program for four years. On the back end, he was going to make sure he was taking care of his people.

You've read stories similar to this throughout this book. When something good happens to you, he has this way of acting like he knew it was going to happen all along. And he had that same reaction with me when I got that job. A twenty-two-year-old kid, having never played college basketball, got a job as an assistant on a Division I staff? It felt like the longest shot ever. To Coach, though, it was inevitable. He knew it.

That gives you supreme confidence. He kept tabs on me, from Holy Cross, to the University of Florida, to 2014, when I took a job in Oklahoma City as the head coach of Thunder's G-League affiliate. He was just so proud and happy, each step of the way. And by then, so was I, because now I got to fulfill my lifelong dream of leading a team.

The coach-player relationship boils down to trust, and the ingredients of trust from a coach's standpoint are competence, consistency, and player-first intentions. Does the coach know what they're doing?

Do I know what I can expect from them day to day? And are they willing to put me and my teammates above themselves? In my opinion, these are the subconscious questions every player asks when I am coaching them.

Now, I cannot coach like Jim Calhoun, but his players trusted him, and that's what I strive for. He made them do it right, do it better, do it harder, do it faster. And while the street fighter in him sometimes had him squaring up with his players, he fought ten times harder when it came to having their backs. He loved them every step of the way. And he did that every single day. It was a simple formula, but greatness isn't complicated.

When you look back at his teams, they weren't assembled behind some kind of template. His best teams didn't always have a roster full of McDonald's All-Americans. But Coach was getting another gear out of his players. It was more than the pushing, the demanding, the hard practices and the drills—it was the psychology. The urgency. The empowerment. I still feel that to this day.

On November 11, 2020, the Oklahoma City Thunder named me their head coach, and Jim Calhoun couldn't wait to talk to me. I looked down at my phone during the craziness of that day, and I had three missed calls from him. First chance I got, I called him back.

I had just been hired as an NBA head coach, probably the most unlikely thing that could have ever happened in my life, and he was calling to tell me he knew it would happen all along. And on a day when I thought I couldn't have felt more empowered by anything, I felt even more empowered. To this day, he makes me feel like I have that extra gear, like I could follow Walter all the way into Manhattan all over again without putting a mark on his Ford Expedition. Like the wind is in my sails.

Coach talks to me now like a peer, and I don't know that I even deserve that. If you simulated my life a million times over, this outcome would have only happened once. I look at all these experiences: the opportunities, the timing, the luck. If you change one turn, I would have ended up in a completely different location, and certainly not coaching an NBA team.

At the first turn, Coach Calhoun gave me access to what it should look like. When you coach a team, you're coaching it against a vision. If that vision is inaccurate, incomplete, or too low of a bar, then you are aiming at the wrong target. I've had access to environments of excellence, and being at UConn with Coach was my first experience with that. I still remember the first practice I saw at UConn, watching him coach. The team was stacked with great players—Emeka, Ben, Taliek—and he was firing on all cylinders, and so was his staff. It was almost poetic.

When you've never seen anything like it, and that's the first thing you see, it sets the bar high. It was a coaching North Star, a reference point that I'm still learning from and reflecting upon, one that I still carry with me in my life and in my coaching. It's the bus that I'm tailing as my own journey unfolds.

Coach Calhoun is a badass, and he'll let you know it. He'll flex that muscle, but then he'll put that muscle behind you. You feel the urgency. The empowerment. The belonging. And the wind fills your sails. Because if you're one of his guys, you're one of his guys.

That's his superpower.

ACKNOWLEDGMENTS

This was meant to be a book not about the game of basketball, but about the people that for me have made it more than a game. So I would be remiss if I didn't mention and thank the many people who have helped me, touched me, along my journey. There are too many for me to mention them all by name, but you know who you are, and you are appreciated. I will never forget you.

All my teachers and coaches in Braintree who helped a young man dealing with a terrible loss, angry for a time at the world, to find his way, and my coaches and professors at American International College.

At Old Lyme, where a wise Connecticut state trooper named Pat Tully helped guide me in my first coaching job. There, and at Westport and Dedham High in Massachusetts, my colleagues and all the young men who allowed me to come into their lives, and came into mine.

At Northeastern, all the assistant coaches on my staff and the players who put their faith in a young coach.

At UConn, where AD John Toner and president John Casteen gave me the opportunity that changed my life in 1986, and helped me to impact a lot of others over the next twenty-six years. People like Lew Perkins, an AD who told me to "think big-time, be big-time"; Ted Taigen, our academic advisor; and Dave Kaplan, Karen Gigliotti, and Katie McMahon, all so invaluable; assistant coaches Dave Leitao (who followed me from Northeastern), Howie Dickenman, Tom Moore, Ted Woodward, Glen Miller, and so many others. And the hundreds of players who gave me the chance to coach them. I hope I helped change their lives for the better, as each of them did for me.

At the University of Saint Joseph, president Rhona Free, among others, convinced me to come out of retirement and helped make coaching basketball, and coaching people, fun all over again. Bernie Schilberg, a man for all seasons, offered unrelenting support at UConn and Saint Joe's.

And to the thousands of fans that make up what is now known as UConn Nation: Every smile, every cheer, even the jeers, helped give a purpose to what we were doing. We built a culture of caring at UConn, and you were part of that.

If I've missed you, again, rest assured you are remembered and appreciated. This story couldn't have been written without you. Thank you, and God bless you all.

Credit: UConn

APPENDIX I

Jim Calhoun's Hall of Fame Induction Speech

In September 2005, Jim Calhoun was inducted into the Naismith Basketball Hall of Fame in Springfield, Massachusetts, the city in which he began his basketball career as a player at American International College. Calhoun was presented by Bob Cousy, and inducted alongside coaches Jim Boeheim and Hubie Brown and the great Brazilian women's star Hortência Maria de Fátima Marcari. Longtime LSU women's coach Sue Gunter was inducted posthumously.

More than fifty of Coach's former and current players were in attendance that night. Here are Jim Calhoun's remarks, in full:

Well, I'd like to start off by saying hello and good-bye, because between Hubie Brown and Jim Boeheim, they told me I had 12 seconds...

Like Hubie and, at times, Jim, I can be rather lengthy. So I wrote this because of the emotion of the evening, the emotion because so many people who have made a significant difference in my life are here. I've tried to avoid names because I'm going to leave someone out who made a significant difference, and that's so difficult to do. This is the hardest speech I ever wrote because this is the greatest honor I've ever received.

I would also like to tell Jim, he looks a little fatigued right now, and tomorrow will be a difficult day, then Sunday he has to try to go visit a kid. The good news is, Tom Moore, our assistant, ran up about five minutes ago. *The kid committed to us.* You're free on Sunday! Congratulations.

...Never give an Irishman the last microphone.

I'd like to begin by thanking The Basketball Hall of Fame and congratulating my fellow inductees. Being inducted with Sue, Hubie, the greatest women's player ever [Hortência Maria de Fátima Marcari]—when Hubie Brown says you're the greatest ever, you must be. And of course, Jim Boeheim, my great friend, who has been something really, really special. Sue Gunter, 708 wins, I don't care where you are, what you're doing, 708 wins is a very special, significant achievement, and obviously she's a special person. I'd like to congratulate each and every one of you for your accomplishments, for it's truly an honor to be in your presence this evening. I'd also like to have all of us remember the lifelong achievement of the late Sue Gunter. I don't think it could have been expressed better than it was, and it certainly brought tears to my eyes.

I'd like to thank Mr. Basketball, Bob Cousy, a man I have so much respect for because I watched him play and I found how—I don't know if the word "conservative" would the right word to describe Bob, but I think that's at least in the right vein—but yet the flashiest and greatest player I ever saw with a basketball. He did things that guys think they can do now. And that's true. He did things, not for show, but for efficiency, and I think you saw, when your name is Mr. Basketball, that's all you need to know. I want to thank Bob for his friendship, his kind words. He has been such a wonderful representative and meant it to so many of us in New England, as a matter of fact, throughout the world. I thank you, Bob, for all your support, friendship throughout the years.

The rest of this is all written because I have a difficult time; occasionally I ramble. My players will attest to that. And they don't have to be here tonight, but Emeka Okafor is right, I can't punish them, I can only praise them, and that's what I want to do tonight.

I want to do it tonight by talking about a game. A game I've been blessed with. A game that has consumed me so much. Basketball is a game that doesn't care what color your skin is, doesn't care what language you speak, what religion you practice. It doesn't care if you're big or small, fast or slow. It simply asks you to play, to compete, to lose with dignity, to win with humility, to make your teammates look good, and to respect your opponent. The game asks that you work to improve, that you put something into it and you give something back to it. The game is universal; it is a language that unites all of us.

The game has taken me, personally, to places I had only dreamed of, and to places I never knew existed. From Braintree High School to American International College here in Springfield, Massachusetts. From Old Lyme, Connecticut, to Westport, Massachusetts. From Boston to Israel, Dedham to Alaska, Sarajevo to Storrs, Connecticut. From the noise of the inner city to the quiet of a sleepy country town. This game has brought me east to west, north to south. The game has introduced me to its citizens, to its ambassadors, to its family, and to its culture. Along the way this game has blessed me with many friends, with many colleagues, with many mentors. I'd be remiss if I didn't mention a few of those: my great high school coach, Fred Herget, [AIC president] Dr. Harry Courniotes, Bob Cousy, John Wooden, Red Auerbach, Dave Gavitt, Bob Knight, John Toner, Dean Smith, and Dee Rowe, and so many others who have helped me chart my course.

And now the game has taken me back to Springfield, and I am so deeply honored, and humbled, to be in such a sacred place and in the presence of such company. One day would not be long enough to thank all the people who have helped me, but I will try to give you a little glimpse tonight. To my wife, Pat, my best friend for thirty-nine years, and the greatest love a man could ever have. You never were the woman behind me, you were always the woman beside me, and I love you.

To my sons, Jim and Jeff—no father could be prouder, and no father could love you any more than I do. To my daughters-in-law, Jennifer and Amy, you are the daughters I never had, and now the daughters that I love. And to my grandchildren, Emily, Katie, Avery, Reese, Sam, and Peyton, you are the light in my world. You bring me a special sort of love. Thank you for everything, my family, thank you for allowing me to be Jim, Dad, Coach, and yeah, Papa. To my mom and dad, Katherine and Jim, who were so special in my life, thank you for your never-ending guidance. To my brother, Bill, my sisters Rose, Margaret, Kathy, and Joan, thank you for your love, not only now, but through my entire life. And to my extended family, and friends, your support—you'll never know how much it's meant to me. Thank you.

To special friends who helped make this night possible, Tim Tolokan and George Blaney, I want to say something to you: simply, thanks.

To all of my assistant coaches, thank you for your passion, thank you for your commitment, and thank you for the honor of sitting on the bench alongside you. (I should change that a little bit, because I haven't sat on the bench in thirty years.)

To the staffs and the administrations at Northeastern University and the University of Connecticut, I thank you for your support and your belief in the profession of teaching, because we, as coaches, are teachers.

To all the unappreciated coaches of New England who have gone before me, and will come after me, who haven't been put in the spotlight as I have been fortunate enough to be, thank you. Thank you for giving me, and the game, so much. I stand here tonight as one of you.

To all the fans, thank you for your passion, thank you for your caring. Thank you for welcoming me, and believing in our kids and in our program.

And lastly, and most importantly for any coach, I want to thank my players. I've had the privilege of coaching you, and you have filled my life with so many memories and so many treasures, some, you'll never know. No coach could ever be successful without players, and as I receive this honor tonight, I want you to know that I take a piece of each and every one of you—and there are over fifty here tonight—into The Hall with me. For you have allowed me to enter The Hall of Fame. You have given of yourself, you have dared to dream, you have enriched my life, and you have made this special game even more beautiful. And if you will indulge me for a moment, I'd like my players in the room, from Dedham High School, we have eight kids from my Dedham High School team back in the late 1960s and '70s, all the way to my present team here, please stand just for a moment.

If you ask me, how I got here and why I coach, there's your answer. God bless you, and good night.

APPENDIX II

Letters for Dad

Family is a concept that means the world to Coach Jim Calhoun. Times change, records are broken, but standards don't change, and the importance of family never wanes. His players over the course of more than fifty years in coaching are his extended family.

His sons, Jim and Jeff, penned these tributes about forty years apart. His oldest, Jim, wrote his as a 14-year-old prep school student. His youngest, Jeff, wrote this tribute for this book, looking back at the unique relationship that grew from playing for his father at UConn.

The coach wanted to include these in *More Than a Game*.

By Jim Calhoun

Why is it that sons always kiss their mothers and only shake hands with their fathers?

After all, men shake hands with other people they hardly know. Does this say that we don't love our fathers as much as our mothers?

No, of course not. I think it says the opposite. Our society has brought us up, as men, not to display our emotions for our fathers until we reach a certain age, where I guess it is okay.

I remember when I was about four years old, my dad told me the story of a little boy who used to kiss his dad good night every night, until one night he forgot to kiss his father. On the morning that followed, the little boy's father was dead. Every night I kiss my dad good night and, just to be sure, I kiss him good-bye every morning.

Throughout my life so far, my dad has supported me in everything I've done. He might not always have agreed with me, but he always supported. During my life, there will be hard times and I know my dad will be there. I know whatever the problem, when all is said and done, I've got my family. That is why I take the love between my dad and me seriously and without reservations. It is important to me that my dad knows I love him. My grandfather died when my father was only fourteen. I know how sad and hurt and alone he is even today. That is why I try to show my love for my dad. If I could accomplish one thing in this world, I'd want to make my dad proud of me and show him how much I love him.

Many people try to disassociate themselves from their family because they think they would rather be with their own friends. I've done this on numerous occasions, and sometimes it is "more fun" to be with kids my own age. But what I, along with many others, sometimes fail to see is that after my high school friendships are over, my dad will still be there. No matter what happens, my family will always be there to love and comfort me.

Deep down inside of me, there is a love for my father which neither I nor he know about. I know it is true because I love him so much and I am very proud of my father.

There is a certain bond of love between a father and a son which is much different from any other. This love can sometimes be buried behind the walls of false "man image." Way down deep, though, there is something unique, which makes the love between my father and me so special.

Two years ago, while my parents were in the living room, my brother and I were finishing dinner in the kitchen. Like all brothers, we exchanged antagonistic words and tried to annoy the other. Then the words became more. I remember feeling an intense pain in my shins after Jeff kicked me. "You little bastard!" I screamed as I lunged for his face. My dad, who had been standing in the doorway unnoticed by us, caught me before I reached his taunting expression.

The so-called "fraternal bond" between Jeff and me had recently grown further and further apart and the fights had become regularities. Dad, who is not home very often because of his job, had had enough of these bouts. "I'm sick and tired of you two fighting. I'm not home very often, and when I do come home, all I get is you two fighting." His angered adrenalin was now pumping furiously through his body, and for a second he lost control. He grabbed me and pushed me into the side of the refrigerator. As I stumbled off-balance, I tripped and fell into, or rather through, the window. I picked myself up and just stared at him for what seemed like an eternity. Wiping blood from my upper lip, I too lost control. "Get the hell away from me!"

I remember running upstairs and crying endlessly as the blood dripped onto my blood-sponged bed. *I hate him*, I thought. *I'm never going to speak to him again*. I was thinking the same thoughts as a fourteen-year-old as I had when my father had punished me as an eight-year-old. It's funny that no matter how old one gets, those thoughts never seem to change much.

The next day my dad and I did talk. We talked about many things but, most importantly, about growing up. His words soothed the pain I had felt the night before. I forgave him and he forgave me.

Deep down inside of me, the depth of my existence, relies on the mutual and unique love and understanding between my family and me. Deep down inside, my dad is my role model. He is my father. He is my best friend.

By Jeff Calhoun

Jim Calhoun was my coach, and he was my dad. That wasn't always easy, during the time I was with him at UConn, for me to tell which one he was, and it probably wasn't easy for him to tell which one I needed him to be.

I was injured pretty much my whole college career, and it was difficult on our relationship. Eventually, it brought us closer. But at the time it created a separation because he was my coach, and he was hard on me, but he's also my dad. You want your dad at times, but there is this distance between coach and player that always exists.

So that time of playing for him was very confusing. I wouldn't say his name in practice. I don't want to say "Coach," I was never going to call him "Dad." So I'd just walk over to him if I needed to talk to him. I didn't know who was in front of me.

When I first got on campus I had to have a shoulder reconstruction. My second year, I'm playing well in preseason and I tear my MCL in my knee. The third year, my other shoulder goes and I'm gone for the year.

I just kept getting hurt, and it affected me mentally. My junior year, I'm struggling in every way. I'm struggling in school. I had never been through depression, didn't know what it looked like, and all of a sudden I didn't want to get up, didn't want to get out of bed.

I was low, and I went in and talked to him; he asked what was going on with me and—immediately—he became my father. He asked what's going on and I said, "I don't know, I'm miserable, I don't want to get out of bed," and he changed. I could see it on his face. I walked in not knowing what to expect, but I needed the dad and he saw it, and we had a father-son talk.

People see him yelling, and he's a hard guy to play for, but the reason he could do it was because everybody on that team knew how much he cared. He knows what people need, he's very in tune, very aware of people and how they're feeling.

Most coach's sons are either the best player on the team or a walk-on. It's really hard when you're neither. I had plenty of Division I offers, and I tried to tell myself I wasn't going to UConn, but when he came up to me after I'd won an award in high school and said, "This isn't coming from me. I told my assistants if they weren't all in agreement we wouldn't do it, but they all said they'd like you to come to UConn." I wondered if I would always ask myself "what if?" When he offered me a scholarship, I knew that I was going to do it.

The things I thought would be issues weren't; the things I didn't see coming were the hard things. Would it be normal with my teammates? I had just been "one of the guys" on every team I'd played on. He did me a favor. He was really, really hard on me. I would be sitting there asking, "Why is he so hard on me?" I know he was trying to make a point, and my teammates knew I had it worse and they rallied around me, protected me. They knew I was one of them, and I wouldn't tell my father anything I wouldn't have told another coach. When the other players were pissed at him, I probably wanted to say what they were saying.

He was very clear I would be treated like everyone else, and he lived up to it. One year I was able to play, I'd get in when we were down and needed some 3s. We were playing St. John's at The Garden and I caught a pass that was going out of bounds; I had to reach back for it. No time on the shot clock, I had to jack it; a kid flying by got a piece of it and it fell short. We lost, and he comes in the locker room, looks right at me, and said, "If you got your butt in the gym more and shot, you'd be ready for the moment when it comes."

And I'm sitting there; I thought I did a good job catching the ball before it went out of bounds. We were down 8 or 9 when I got in with like a minute and a half to go, and we were down 8 or 9 and I'm the first guy he gets on.

I was injured and never got the chance to show it, but I knew I belonged. That was always my frustration. When he told me recently that he should have played me more, it gave me a peace.

I'm extremely proud when players call and ask him for advice about being a father. He always picks up the phone, even for guys who didn't leave on the best terms. More than the championships and the wins and the Hall of Fame, the stuff I see that he's done for people, no selfish part of it, not for anyone to know, that is the thing I'm most proud of. His caring. He has a need to help people, he needs to be needed. And his capacity for it is limitless.

After our father-son talk in his office, I decided I had to get away. I went to Miami for a semester, though I later returned to get my degree at UConn. He took me to the airport, this was when you could go through security even if you weren't flying. I didn't want to leave, but I felt I had to. He walked me to the gate, and he quickly said good-bye and I knew he was crying. I don't think I'd ever seen him cry. He's this tough guy and he's bigger than life, but his humanity is just...he's just a special guy.

And I knew that at the end of the day, I always had him. I've spent my life being his son; I played for him, I coached with him at Saint Joe's, and he's pretty much my best friend. I'm pretty lucky to know him, and to understand him, on all those sides.

ABOUT THE AUTHOR

Jim Calhoun, born in Braintree, Massachusetts, played basketball at American International College and later coached at Old Lyme High in Connecticut, Westport and Dedham High in Massachusetts, at Northeastern University, UConn, and the University of Saint Joseph. He won three NCAA titles with UConn and was inducted into the Naismith Hall of Fame. He and his wife, Pat, live in Connecticut and have two sons and six grandchildren.

Dom Amore, born in New Haven, Connecticut, is the sports columnist at the *Hartford Courant*. He has been writing about sports in Connecticut since 1982, has won more than thirty state and national journalism awards, and has been named the state's sportswriter of the year seven times by the National Sports Media Association.